Jack Benny, George Burns, Milton Berle, Bob Mitchum, Ann Miller and others have told stories about *Benny Rubin* on television. Now read how it REALLY was with William Randolph Hearst at San Simeon — Orson Welles' crash into Hollywood — Max Baer's conquests in Society — Intimate stories about Lucille Ball, Charlie Chaplin, Sinatra, Capone, Berle, Haley, Cantor, Jolson, Keeler, Jessel, Thomas, Ziegfeld and many more — in his book **COME BACK-STAGE WITH ME.** Order it from your book dealer NOW! Only $4.95 clothbound.

COME BACKSTAGE WITH ME

COME BACKSTAGE WITH ME

By

Benny Rubin

Bowling Green University Popular Press
Bowling Green, Ohio 43403

ISBN: 0-87972-040-9

Dedicated to my daughters Lyla and Donna

No father has known more love.

CONTENTS

COME BACKSTAGE WITH ME

BENNY RUBIN IS NOT ONLY A GENUINELY
FUNNY MAN, HE IS A PERCEPTIVE SHOW-BUSINESS
HISTORIAN. IT IS IMPORTANT THAT HE HAS
TRANSMITTED TO US HIS FIRST-HAND KNOWLEDGE
OF THE WORLD OF ENTERTAINMENT.

Steve Allen

I HAVE BEEN LAUGHING AT BENNY RUBIN TELLING STORIES FOR FIFTY YEARS. IF THAT SOUNDS PARADOXICAL BECAUSE I AM ONLY THIRTY-NINE, THAT WAS BEFORE I WAS RE-INCARNATED TO THIS AGE.

KNOWING HIM ALL OF THOSE YEARS, I STILL LAUGH AT HIM BECAUSE HE JUST DOESN'T TELL A STORY, HE LIVES THE PEOPLE. DURING THE TIME HE WORKED WITH ME ON MORE THAN FOUR HUNDRED RADIO AND TELEVISION SHOWS, I HAVE ASKED HIM TO WRITE JUST THIS KIND OF A BOOK, AND I AM EXTREMELY HAPPY THAT HE HAS.

IF HE HAS INCLUDED—AND HE SAID HE HAS—STORIES ABOUT US IN CHICAGO, KANSAS CITY, NEW YORK AND OUR YEARS AT M.G.M., YOU ARE IN FOR A TREAT! . . . MARY AND GEORGE BURNS ARE IN A GREAT MANY OF THEM.

MY REPUTATION IS THAT I AM CHEAP, RIGHT? YOU MAY USE THIS AS A LEGAL DOCU-MENT; I AM GOING TO BUY THE BOOK . . . WHOLESALE.

Jack Benny

I HAVEN'T READ BENNY RUBIN'S BOOK,
BUT I CERTAINLY WILL BECAUSE HE'S ALWAYS
BEEN ONE OF OUR GREAT STORY TELLERS—
BESIDES, MY NAME IS ON THE JACKET.

George Burns

BENNY RUBIN IS ONE OF GOD'S CHOSEN PEOPLE. WHY, BECAUSE HE'S JEWISH? NO. BECAUSE HE'S MADE MILLIONS OF PEOPLE LAUGH; MADE THEM HAPPY.

HOW DO I KNOW? BECAUSE FOR FORTY-FIVE YEARS HE'S BEEN MAKING ME LAUGH AS A FRIEND, AS A GAG MAN ON MY SCRIPTS, AND AS AN ACTOR IN MY FILMS.

AND NOW BENNY HAS PUT HIS UNIQUE FUNNY-STORY-TELLING TALENTS INTO A BOOK SO THAT MANY MORE MILLIONS OF EARTH PEOPLE MAY GO ON LAUGHING WITH BENNY LONG AFTER HE GRADUATES TO A HIGHER CIRCUIT.

P.S. MAY IT BRING YOU MAZEL AND MAMMA AND MOOLA.

Frank Capra

HIS HIGHNESS SPEAKS TO HIS LOWNESS.

MY DEAR YOUNG BENNY,

YOU PAY ME A COMPLIMENT, SIR, IN ASKING ME TO WRITE A PREFACE TO YOUR BOOK, BUT I MUST SAY, "NO."

FOR ONE THING, YOUR BOOK IS ONE OF HUMOR, AND AS YOU KNOW, I LIVED IN ENGLAND FROM 1894 TO 1926 AND ALTHOUGH IN THIS YEAR OF GRACE, 1972, I RETAIN SOME OF MY SENSES, THE ONE OF HUMOR IS NOT AMONG THEM. BESIDES, I AM RETIRED. . . VOLUNTARILY, I MAY ADD . . . WHICH MEANS I DO NOTHING. NOW TO DO NOTHING AND LIKE IT IS AN ART IN ITSELF, BUT TO WRITE A PREFACE I CONSIDER DOING SOMETHING, WHICH WOULD UPSET THE GLORIOUS RHYTHM OF DOING NOTHING.

YOUR BOOK CONSISTS OF HUMOROUS STORIES AND SITUATIONS WHICH ARE VERY ENTERTAINING, BUT HOW DO YOU REMEMBER THESE THINGS? I WAS AN ALLEGED ACTOR FOR FIFTY-FOUR YEARS, AND ALL I CAN REMEMBER IS TO SAY THE WORDS, GET THE MONEY, AND PISS OFF (ENGLISH EXPRESSION MEANING "BUGGUR-OFF). IF I HAD THE TIME AND THE INCLINATION, TO DO AS YOU ASK, IT WOULD TAKE PAGES AND PAGES OUT OF MY LIFE AND YOUR BOOK. I SHOULD HAVE TO TELL IN DETAIL OF YOUR GETTING ME TO SERVE TEA TO THE PLAYERS IN A BASEBALL GAME, YOUR PENCHANT FOR BREAKING THE BACKS OF OUR CHAIRS, AND YOUR AVID DESIRE FOR LOATH– SOME CEREAL AT THREE A.M. NO, DEAR BOY, CAN'T DO IT.

VIRGINIA SENDS HER LOVE TO YOU AND YOUR PAPERBACKS, AND I, BEING A SNOB, SEND MY LOVE TO YOU AND YOUR STIFF COVERS.

AFFECTIONATELY,

Arthur (Pip, to you) Treacher

THE ALLEY AIN'T WHAT IT USED TO BE

Oh, it's still there, but the stage entrance isn't. Sure, the door is there, but it's sealed up so literally there is no stage entrance. There are no actors to go through it, or stage Johnnies to hang around it. The little sign is there, but the light globe above it has been removed.

On the inside, the door is meaningless too. The doorkeeper isn't around to tell you you can't come in, because nobody comes in. And those who are allowed to come in, don't. There is somebody in there, but he walks down the aisle of the place to get there. He is a stagehand—singular.

There isn't a pinochle game going on so there are no stagehands—plural. He plays hands all right, but that comes later. This fellow's job is to dim the lights and press a button that opens the front traveler (drape curtain). When the drape unfurls itself, the movie goes on, *then* he plays cards—solitaire. He's got from six to eight hours to play "Canfield," or any game he wants. He can put a nine on a king, or a black on a black, and there's nobody to catch him cheating, because there is no more stage entrance for the other guys to come through.

Nobody anxiously asks the doorman for mail, for there is no doorman and the mailman couldn't get through the stage door anyway . . . and no one to deliver mail to.

No one calling for "props," no one yells, "half hour" or "fifteen minutes," or "who's the louse that took my *Variety*?" The familiar, "Pipe down the sketch is on," is heard no more. And, "Where the hell is Jan? He's on next." There is no one to get him out of the bar on the corner.

The bar is still there, but there is no bright conversation between the newspaper guys. They couldn't hear each other anyway, with that juke box blaring. There is no one to answer, "How
the hell do I know where I go next week? I haven't heard from
my agent!"

Downstairs, you cannot hear the thumping and grunts of the
acrobats warming up, or the tuning up of the orchestra.

It's strange not to hear the sister act fighting, or that louse
with the banjo breaking your eardrums.

And there's the animal room that housed "Fink's Mules,"
"Powers' elephants," the "Gaudschmidt's dogs and ponies,"
"Swaynes cats and rats," and the many dog acts. But the room
isn't empty, there are animals in there—rats.

I even miss the "touches," and the guys who promote phony
benefits; the song pluggers, the guys who hustled you for "ads,"
even the laundries that broke the buttons on your shirts.

But the Alley; never again will it be graced with Jack Benny
entering it jauntily with his fiddle under his arm, Bob Hope with
his golf clubs, Phil Baker and accordion, Cliff Edwards with his
"Uke," Bill Demarest and his cello, Jack Haley with his bank
books, Jim Barton riding a bicycle, Frisco and his cigar, Ben Bernie,
Gracie hugging George's arm, Jessel with a chick, Cantor humming
"Margie" and Gus Edwards handing out coins to every kid there.

Of course, there was Berle with his mother, Sandra; the Marx
Brothers and Mother Minnie; Peter Lind Hayes and Mama Grace;
Elsie Janis and her ma; Buster Keaton and his pa; Willie Howard
and his brother Eugene; Bert Wheeler eating an apple; Lou Holtz
with the *Wall Street Journal*; the Creole fashion plate carrying his
dresses; song writer Harry Ruby wearing a fielders glove with a
baseball in it; Will Rogers' smiling face with a gob of gum in it.
Naturally there was Sophie Tucker and Ted Snyder, Blossom
Seeley and Benny Fields, Jimmy Durante being hugged by Clayton
and Jackson, Harry Houdini struggling with his trunk key on his
key ring, Fred Allen with his Portland, the loveable Smith and
Dale.

However, the Alley is being used for other celebrities who
grace it with their presence. There is Sam Tranafats, who with the
one and only Tom Twirvy make their presence known twice a
week when Sam deftly picks up the cans of garbage and heaves

them into the truck. Then Tom daintily presses a lever that makes the back end come up ever so slowly, to press the cargo up front. Then, just as tenderly, regresses the back end into a position for Sam's next deposit. This is artistry at its epitomy!

I miss the Alley.

THERE'S AN ALLEY IN THIS YARN TOO

In 1925 I signed a contract that made my heart flutter and my hand shook so I could hardly manage my signature. It was for a show called *No Foolin* and the dream of all comics, it was to appear for Mr. Florenz Ziegfeld.

We played a week in Atlantic City and went to New York.

Came the dress rehearsal the night before opening in New York. Mr. Ziegfeld had many millionaire backers there, plus newspapermen and agents for some of the actors in the show. Songs, sketches and girl numbers were going on and off smoothly. It was time for my second appearance and Gene Buck said to me, "This is going to make you, kid." I thanked him. Then he gave me a joke that would fit a railroad station sketch I was about to do. "Isn't that a bit risque?" I asked. He told me that I was not in vaudeville now. On Broadway you could say anything! I rehearsed the joke to myself.

A big musical and girl number finished and all the beautiful ladies joined the others in the audience to see the sketch. Because once we were open they'd be making costume changes and this was their only chance to see the show. The first few lines got good laughs and I chuckled inwardly. "Oh, will those comics on Forty-Seventh Street eat their hearts out!" Then came the new joke and no sooner was it out of my mouth than Mr. Ziegfeld yelled, "That's enough of that kind of joke." I tried to explain and he yelled, "Get off the stage."

Three times that happened and I finally blew my stupid top. I said, "Look, Mr. Ziegfeld, I played the finest theatres in America and always made good money. So you quit yelling at me!" He ignored me and called to his stage manager, Zeke Colvin, "Next number, Zeke!"

I went into the alley still wearing my trainman's uniform. My resentment boiled. "How do you like that? Wouldn't even let me explain! MM! Well, someone will come out here soon and say 'You're due to do your specialty next and you'd better get ready!' Or someone else will say, 'Listen, kid, you've made a mistake, now go back and apologize and you'll be all right!' Well, if someone is coming to say anything, where are they? Maybe after this number someone will come out."

But nobody came. No one. The show opened the next night on schedule *without* me and as far as anyone is concerned I'm still out there in the alley.

YESTERDAY

Vaudevillians always remember the unimportant—themselves. The poet Hazlitt described us as "the only honest hypocrites." I'm the best example of that and I'll prove it.

I have spent more than fifty years living and reliving this illiterature. So, if you want to have some fun by living a little yesterday, be my guest and come backstage with me.

That doesn't mean that I'm going to compare anything or anybody with the good old days. They were really lousy.

How about having a sandbox right in the house? It used to take four and a half days on a train to go from here to New York. Now it's four and a half hours. Who needs a restaurant that served yesterday's cold roast beef with today's hot gravy when a glorious TV dinner is only six bits? You had to be a millionaire to own wheels. Now it's only a few bucks down and changing the address. I got sixty dollars a week as a star in a burlesque show doing fourteen two and a half hour performances a week. Now I get sixty five by just standing in line.

If you're one of those people who think oldtimers were better than the kids of today, you'll get no argument from me, because I ain't alistenin'.

Before I proceed, let me lay this one on you. Any chorus girl, or boy, today can out-dance any dancing star of yesterday you can name.

Since language and semantics will guide you through a lot of this, let's get at it.

My first language was the salty jargon of the poor in the streets and alleys of Boston, Massachusetts.

Polite society called our jive vile, vulgar and filthy. This same language is now identified with the Broadway stage, movies and books. However, it is termed classical.

From playing on amateur nights, I learned a new kind of vernacular.

The flooring of the first ten feet of a stage was called "the boards."

The space—the apron or down in one.

The curtain that backed that area—a drop.

Eight feet back of that was—two.

All the space back of two was—full stage.

Footlights—the foots.

Entrance and exits—the wings.

The arch that encircled the stage—the proscenium.

The high place the scenery was flown to—the flies.

A bit hit—we killed 'em or laid them in the aisles.

Failure—flop.

Good audience—red hat (meaning the audience would even laugh at grotesque wardrobe).

Bad audience—we were over their heads.

My first contact with professionalism came from Johnny Sullivan, with whom I worked, and came to know, on amateur nights. His stage name was Fred Allen.

All I had ever seen him do was juggle, but when he let me come backstage and watch him from the wings, he talked too. The audience howled at him, but I didn't dig the jokes. You see, this guy read books, while I was in reform school learning how to steal.

If you remember the soft-spoken intellectual Fred, he was the same as a kid. But paradoxically, hc could fight like hell.

Plus his juggling and my wooden shoe dancing, we both boxed three rounds for three bucks. He had—and won—fifty-one consecutive fights. I had thirty and blew them all.

Not long after that, I too became a pro, when my limited talents reached out and stole the money. (January twenty-ninth, nineteen hundred and fourteen.)

The fellow that gave me my first job was Lou Walters of "Latin Quarter" fame.

There was a year in a "tab" show, one season on a showboat

on the Ohio River, then small-time vaudeville.

The troupe I was with on the showboat was called a "tab" show. The kids starting today should get a load of this before they beef about only getting a few hundred a week.

The average show had ten people in it. Four men (had to be a quartet), and six girls, one of whom could sing a solo and then step back into the line and dance with the others.

If a town was large enough, they could play a week, (six days). If not, they changed "bills" every day. Consequently, you had a crack at playing every kind of a character—and learning.

An example of how to store the goodies of the other guy's experiences.

The "business" end of a tab show was as follows:

The theatre paid the owner two hundred and fifty dollars a week against a percentage. What? Yes! for the whole show. This, now, was the "nut" (expense) for the owner:

Three male actors	$15.00 per week each
Six girls	75.00 (for all six)
Piano Player	20.00
Railroad fares	50.00 (never over $5.00 each)
Baggage hauling	25.00
Pay-off on wardrobe	5.00
Pay-off on scenery	10.00

The gross amount of expenses was never over this two hundred, so the owner had fifty dollars (sixty-two fifty if his wife worked), and a crack at the percentages.

To qualify for that fifteen bucks a week, I out-danced five hoofers, sang the lead with the quartet, played two tunes on the trombone (learned in reform school) and juggled (I was taught by Fred Allen).

Room and board was six bucks a week (two bits extra if you wanted wood for the pot-belly stove in the bedroom). I sent my Ma five and had a ball with the other four bucks.

The first joke about vaudeville I heard was when the grieving comic at the grave of his wife looked at the few mourners and asked, "Is there a straight man in the crowd who knows the Lord's

Prayer?"

People under thirty-five are led to believe that vaudeville was played in a honky tonk theatre with a five-piece orchestra.

A typical act was, two guys in straw hats, wearing blazers and carrying canes. They danced to "Tea for Two" and interrupted their soft shoe with—

"Who was that lady I saw you with last night?" "That was no lady, that was my wife." "I saw your father coming out of a saloon." "Well, he had to come out some time."

"I passed your house today."

"Thank you."

". . . and I saw you kissing your wife."

"It just shows what a dope you are, I wasn't home today."

The people who do that as their version of what vaudeville was couldn't have made it. In fact, most of them couldn't have gotten past the doorman.

Some of the theatres I played had magnificent architecture, ten to twenty musicians in the pit and that seat you sat in was yours. Some families had them reserved for years.

Please allow me to present just one eight-act bill:

1) The Rath Brothers. Two nice-looking guys with rippling muscles under their silk costume. They performed difficult feats of gymnastics, with no grunts and no appeal for applause.

2) The Wilton Sisters. Two beautifully dressed girls, who sang popular songs with the cadence and beauty of an organ.

3) Robert Warwick. Twenty minutes of drama that sounded like Helen Hayes reading poetry with the impact of a sledge hammer.

4) Val and Ernie Stanton. Two American boys satirizing English Hall comedy. No aim at belly laughs. You just sat there and chuckled with delight.

5) Ruth Etting. Need I say more of that velvet voice?

6) Gus Edwards and his Gang. You had the feeling

of ten "milltowns." As they sang, you hummed to yourself. He put you in heaven for twenty five minutes.

7) Lucky me, with Billy K. Wells material that made people holler.

8) Those that walked out missed a clever dog act, artists on parallel bars, or the precision of Gautiers dogs and ponies.

No, my friends, "Who was that lady I saw you with?" was not big time vaudeville.

Please forgive an old guy taking his hat off in respect.

Sure there was small time, like there is minor league baseball.

=============

The following is some of the small time that you could play: The Gus Sun Time, the Delaney Time, the Delmar Time, the Loew Time, Pantages Circuit, and Western Vaudeville.

In New York there was a man by the name of Fatty Marcus who had small, small time. This was one and two nights. I'll give you an example of the kind of acts he booked, and how he booked them.

Picture yourself on 46th Street standing in a group of small, small time vaudevillians. Almost always you would see them looking toward the heavens, but in reality, their sights were not gunned that high. They were looking up at the windows in the offices of the Fatty Marcuses. The small time booker would yell out the window, "I'll give this for a trio to go to (some small town)." Now, the "this" that he was offering them was one finger for three days (meaning one hundred dollars). Sometimes he only put up his thumb, which meant half of that. I will never forget visiting with these guys one day when Fatty yelled out the window to a dancing team that owned a car, "I'll give you (forefinger and thumb) to play the last half in Torrington, Connecticut, providing you drive the rest of the acts." The actor answered, "I'll take it, if it's downhill."

=============

You don't have to remember vaudeville to realize how important it was to "get off." (For the uninitiated, it means to exit to great applause.)

You see it now on most top TV shows. The singer is a cinch, if he, or she, has a high note.

The dancer gets a lot of help from the orchestra blasting as he does his big step.

The juggler and acrobat rely on the big trick. But what about the comics who can neither sing nor dance? Most of them have the orchestra hit the loudest chord they can, to tell you, "this is it."

The vaudevillian's greatest dilemma wasn't as much the closing as the opening. If they didn't capture the audience in the first minute they had a hell of a time building from there.

Here then are some classic openings of vaudeville acts I played on the bill with:

    JACK BENNY: Hello, my name is Jack Benny.
                  (to orchestra leader) How is
                  the show up to now?
    ORCHESTRA LEADER: Fine
    JACK BENNY: Well, I'll put a *stop* to that.

Curtains open on a scene where you can see absolutely nothing (pitch black) and two men with clipped British accents argue to the point where one man shoots the other. On the loud report of the pistol, the lights come on to find two Negro men lying on the ground, half asleep . . . they did a dancing act.

============

While the orchestra quietly plays the intro to an operatic selection the stagehands roll out a red velvet carpet the full length of the stage. The coloratura voice offstage starts to sing, and when the music and the voice reach the highest crescendo, the dirtiest looking bum you ever saw enters. His name was "Milo." His act was mimickry.

============

The music is Greig's (something delicate and light about morning). The lights come up slowly, as if it was the sun rising. We see a street scene with a few stores. Three of them have awnings over the front rolled up. When the lights are full up, the owner of the store in the center, lowers his awning and a dirty tramp falls out of it. Nat Wills, a monologist.

============

This scene is a beautiful garden. The music is "Roses Are Blooming in Picardy." Roy Cummings enters singing the song in a spotlight. He is handsome. He is wearing a blue jacket and white flannel trousers; when he is about to hit the last high note of the song someone (behind the curtain) pushes him hard and he goes headfirst into the orchestra pit. He comes back up filthy and bedraggled and sings the high note.

============

The curtains part as we hear the good solid rhythm of a jazz band. While there is a good beat, there is good melody and harmony. A violinist rises for an eight-bar solo and hits one clinker that is barely discernible. The violinist seated next to him rises and breaks his fiddle over the guy's head. Frank and Milt Britton.

============

The scene is an apartment house. The spotlight goes from one side of the stage to the other, looking for Shaw and Lee. Eventually the spotlight finds them looking out of a window on the fifth floor. The entire curtain is lowered to the floor with them hanging onto some piece of "rigging." They step over the mass of canvas and go into their comedy act.

============

The scene is winter. Snow falling from the "flies" and wind machines from the sides of the stage conjure up unmerciful cold. Dramatic music makes it even more foreboding. The spotlight

28

goes to stage left and picks up two Negroes (Miller and Lyle) wearing the thinnest of palm beach suits.

After considerable trembling, Miller stutters to Lyle. "Let's take the fifty cents we just made shovelling snow and get some hot soup."

LYLE: I ain't got no fifty cents.

MILLER: I saw the man give it to you.

LYLE: I know, but I spent it.

MILLER: On what?

LYLE: A thermometer.

MILLER: Can we eat it?

LYLE: No, we can't eat it. (takes it out of his pocket) It's glass. Look here.

MILLER: What good is it?

LYLE: What good is it!!! It can tell you how cold it is.

MILLER: Man, I don't need nuthin to tell *me* how cold it is.

LYLE: See these numbers on here? When this red thing gets up to this number, that means put on your overcoat.

MILLER: Is there a number on there that tells you where to get a overcoat at?

LYLE: I can tell you where to get a overcoat ON TIME.

MILLER: You mean *and time.*

============

Comedian Harry Rose would yell from offstage, "Here's Harry," then enter singing. That was when there was "big time," two shows a day vaudeville. When the "band on stage" era moved in, they placed a small runway from the stage over the vacant orchestra pit, to the front railing.

Ed Sullivan introduced "Harry Rose the Broadway Jester!" Rose yelled out his familiar "Here's Harry," ran on stage, and fell into the orchestra pit. (The stagehands had forgotten to set the runway into position.) The band leader yelled down to Harry lying in the pit, "Do you want me to play your introduction again?"

=============

Harris and Holly's opening line was very succinct. Holly struggled, pulling a piano onstage. Bud Harris, barely touched it on the other end.

HOLLY:	Come on, come on, push that thing!
BUD:	You just go on pullin, this end'll follow.

=============

Bill Demarest entered to a classical musical introduction, seated himself center stage and proceeded to play beautifully on a cello. After about sixteen bars, he had become enraptured with the selection, stopped playing suddenly, leaned the cello on the chair, lay flat on his back and tried to do a "nip-up." He failed miserably and landed back on his rump with a whack! His partner "Collete" helped him up and they went on with their comedy act.

=============

Bert Fitzgibbons entered from the audience. As he reached the stage he broke the footlights in front of him with his cane, and said, "Nobody sleeps while I'm on!"

=============

I saved this one for last because it impressed me the most.
The multi-talented man who did this was Fred Stone.
You heard a soft, ominous tone played by the orchestra until the big bang of an explosion came from under the stage. The music reached its highest crescendo, as Mr. Stone's body came hurtling straight up like a rocket. His body was covered with foam

as he landed lightly on his feet.

He said, "I think I put in one raisin too many."

============

Walter Huston (Huston and Rice) went into the audience with a shotgun and dared the audience not to applaud Miss Rice singing.

============

Si Wills of Wills and Davis (Joan Davis) walked center stage and announced "Will the lady in the audience with the lucky ticket come up and get me?"

============

Lorraine Rognan, dressed beautifully, including a lush fur piece on her neck, sang a song and as she bowed to the applause, the fur piece slipped to the floor and walked off. It was a live dog.

============

I'm sorry I don't know the lady's name, but I'll never forget her magnificent voice singing an operatic aria, and as the applause thundered, she raised her long gown, revealing roller skates and she skated off.

============

In my first attempt at vaudeville, I wrote myself a single from all the best things I did in all of the shows and played a few small time dates. Then I got an idea for a big act, but could never promote the money for it. I was living in the Princeton Hotel in New York when my money ran out and I was asked to move. The joint was full of actors and song writers. Fellows like Irving Berlin, Al Bryant who wrote "I Didn't Raise My Boy to be a Soldier," "Daddy," "You've Been More Than A Mother to Me," and many more. Some very famous malaprops were originated in this hotel by Donald Kerr (of Kerr and Weston). He was trying to improve his English and said things like "Pass the sugar if I'm not too inquisitive," "Jump in my car and I'll take you to your destitution." There were three other fellows, Bert Hanlon, Benny Ryan and Violinsky, who just then were writing songs like, "When Frances Dances With Me," "Honolulu Eyes," "Vamping Rose" and some more. They were sympathetic and not only helped me financially, but spoke to Benny Davis, the songwriter (who wrote a thousand hits besides "Margie"). He was putting on the show at the celebrated Reisenweber's Cafe. Reisenweber's had various rooms and played the biggest stars of the time. You only saw famous people at the tables; the average guy couldn't afford the place.

Benny didn't know me or my work and had me come to Reisenweber's for a tryout. He and Mr. Wagner, the manager, sat in judgment of Benny Meroff, Charlie Calvert and myself. Meroff did some exceptional dancing and Charlie was sensational as an acrobatic dancer. I wanted to run out of the joint, because all I could do was taps. But I got up anyway and did every roll and tap I knew how to do. I really gave that floor a beating. Davis and Wagner went into a huddle. I caught my breath and slowly started out, only to be called back. They had decided to have us all work a week and choose the one that was the biggest hit. Meroff would not go for it and left. Charlie and I accepted. When we were told to come to rehearsal and what day we were to open, I asked Davis how I was to dress. He casually told me to wear my tuxedo. What tuxedo? Who owned a tuxedo? Charlie did!

In the street, I made a deal with Charlie to do a double dance, after our singles. I knew I'd be a dead, stinking fish doing taps to a noisy, crowded room. Charlie agreed and I raced to the Princeton with the good news. Ryan and I wore the same size shoes (four and a half) and since he was going to quit acting and devote all of his time to songwriting, he gave me a pair of patent leathers. Incidentally, this is the Ryan of "Ryan and White" (George White of Scandals fame) and Ryan and Lee, the first dumb type girl act. He did retire for awhile, then did an act with Gracie Allen. Bert Hanlon was a big time monologist plus being a hit songwriter. He gave me a dress shirt, collar and links.

Violinsky did a big time act too. He gave me a tuxedo, but

it was too large and I wound up with only the vest. Again Hanlon came through with studs. I called Davis about an advance, so I could rent a tuxedo. He had a better idea. He'd sell me one and I could pay it off, so much a week. I leaped at that proposition; it meant he couldn't let me out after the first week. Oh yes, I forgot to mention that I had enough money to buy a tie.

On opening night I went on with a new song to sing, written specially for me by the three clothes lenders. It was "Vamping Rose" and I'd say about half of the audience heard me. Then the dance. They watched for a moment only; since the music and crowd noise drowned out the taps there was nothing to see and everyone turned to talk to each other. I went off the floor to nothing. Charlie fared much better, he was a great acrobat and the audience watched every move. I knew then I was cooked. Paying Davis for the suit was no guarantee—he had only to take it back and finis. Charlie was a big hit. I didn't wait for the applause to subside, or for him to catch his breath, and motioned to the leader to play St. Louis Blues, our double number. In this dance I did little more than balance Charlie in certain tricks, but it was the hit of the show and we were kept on as a team for nine weeks at seventy-five bucks a week.

Near the end of my run, a fellow named Bal Lloyd sent for me. At his table he explained that he did a blackface act with a man by the name of Welles and they had split up. He had contracts for three unplayed weeks at three hundred a week and would I be his partner. We met for rehearsal next day and where do you think he was living: My hotel. It wasn't so strange that I hadn't ever seen him because Bal worked all the time. He started to tell me the blackface routine and I stopped him and explained that I was much better in white face and had good jokes too. He wasn't easy to sell. Here was a guy, born in Richmond, Virginia, in the United States of America, who couldn't read or write the language and was in show business only because his brother Al (of Aveling and Lloyd) was a big time act. Bal was a dancer, but a faker and had to have a partner that could beat out the taps for both. Now you know the reason he picked me out in the first place. Finally sold him and went to work teaching him white face jokes.

We were booked into the Temple Theatre in Detroit, but it would be murder to open cold. His agent tried and failed to get a one-nighter for us so we could make Detroit. So, we took a three-day stand in Brooklyn. The matinee was pretty good and the supper show better. At the end of the last dance, I faked a trip and did a fall I had learned in burlesque and turned my ankle badly. We couldn't do the last show, but made the train that got us into Detroit in time for rehearsal.

The manager of the Temple invariably sat in the first entrance. During the first show, the audience laughed, but he did not. The audience applauded, but he made no sign. When the show was over, he sent for us. What could he possibly beef about? We were a big hit, no risque material and we signed in relief when we heard his complaint:

The pictures out front were blackface; the name was Welles with Lloyd; why now a white face act and who was Rubin? Quickly, we ad libbed that the booking office made the mistake and we would deliver him white face pictures and billing. We borrowed money from Tom Dugan who headlined, ran to a photographer, posed, waited for the pictures (blew our dinner) and brought them to the manager, slightly moist.

We were a hit. Offers poured into Bal's agent, M. S. Bentham. The salary jumped to three hundred and fifty and we were hailed as the new Gallagher and Shean. When we started to play return dates around Chicago, we were offered the Orpheum Circuit for four fifty. We said "Yes," the agent said "No." New York would hail us and pay seven hundred and fifty or more. He didn't even allow us to play Cleveland, Pittsburgh or Philadelphia on the way in. Those theatres could wait and pay the big salary.

Lloyd and I went into New York and opened at the Alhambra Theatre, fourth on the bill, a perfect spot. Well, we laid the biggest egg you ever saw. The excuse was this: On ahead of us was an artistic gentleman by the name of Richard Keene. He did Shakespearean characterizations which were excellent. But the last guy he did was a miser counting his gold and somehow or another, the money killed him. The last sight of him you saw, before seeing us, was a green spotlight on his kisser, no teeth and his tongue hanging out a foot. Twelve minutes after he died, we did. Our agent wouldn't even come backstage to see us. The booker, I. R. Samuels was for throwing us out. But his assistant, Leo Morrison, came back, gave us a tongue-lashing and put us on second. We perished there too.

The week was over and, how the agent did it we didn't know; but he booked us on the Delmar Time in the South. Maybe Mr. Delmar was sold that we were a good "out-of-town act." And we were.

SOME OF US USED IDENTIFYING LABELS

Ned (Clothes) Norton
Eve (Look at him) Sully
Herb (Spotlight) Williams
Joe (Wanna buy a duck?) Penner
Harry (I think you touch) Burns
Jack (Madman) Rose
Harry (Broadway Jester) Rose
Henry (Squitjulum) Lewis
Dan (Mayor of Broadway) Healy
Ted ("the High Hatted Tagadian") Lewis
Lou (O Solo Mio) Holtz
(Bazooka) Bob Burns
Nat Wills "Shabby Genteel"
Abe (Blutch) Cooper
(Sliding) Billy Watson
Billy (Beef trust) Watson
(Think a drink) Hoffman
(Sliding) Sammy Spears
(Smiling) Sammy Spears
Aveling and Lloyd "Two Gentlemen from the South"
Smith and Dale "Doctor Kronkeit and Hungarian Rhapsody"
Sophie Tucker "The last of the red hot Mamas"
Ray Samuels "The Blue Streak of Vaudeville"
Eddie Leonard "The Minstrel Man"
Bard and Pearl "Baron Munchhausen"
Dezzo Retter "I wrestle with myself"
Harry Langdon "Johnny's new car"
Gallagher and Shean "On the boardwalk"
"Tates Motering"
John B. Hyams "Come on, Red"

Maurice Samuels "The sign of the rose"
Dugan and Raymond "Under the apple tree"
Val and Ernie Stanton "Two English boys from
    America"
Charles Judels "The Pauper and the Princess"
Imhoff, Conn and Corrine "The pest house"
Kenny and Hollis "The Rah Rah boys"
Victor Moore "Change your act or go back to
    the woods"
Charles Chaplin "A Night in an English Music
    Hall"
Gus Edwards "School days"
Eddie Buzzel "Cookies"
Al Herman "The black assassin of mirth"
Phil Baker "A bad boy from a good family"
Benny Rubin "The Yankee Doodle boy"
Joe Laurie, Jr. "The pint-sized author comedian"
Clayton and Edwards "Black and Tan"
Burns and Allen "Lamb chops"
Wells, McGinty and West "The house wreckers"
Swaynes "Cats and Rats"
Powers "Elephants"
Finks "Mules"
Gaudschmidt's "Dogs and Ponies"
"Gautiers Shetland Ponies"
"Wanda and her seal"
Arnaut Brothers (listen to the birdies)
"Captain Schneider's Lions and Tigers"
Billy Williams (Doggone)
"Hank and his educated mule"
Ed Wynn "The perfect fool"
Julius Tannen "The Sophisticate"
Cliff Arquette "A letter from mama"
Abbott and Costello "Who's on first?"
Walter C. Kelly "The Virginia Judge"
Bert Gordon "The mad Russian"
Moran and Mack "Two Black Crows"
Moss and Frye "How high is up?"
Pat Rooney the III "A chip off the old block"

Owen McGivney "Protean Artist"
Bozo Synder "The piano movers"

Can't remember the names of:

"the paper hangers" (one of them was named
    Williams)
"The Arkansas Traveler"
"The last bus" (One name was Connolly)

Harry (Zoup) Welch
Harry (Hello, Jake) Fields

With the average civilian (layman to vaudevillian) they can tell you any date of anything of importance with, "That happened when we got the piano," or "that was right after the baby was born."

Not so with vaudevillians. It either happened "during, before or right after knocking them cold at the Palace."

The Palace was the place to play, talk about, or get booked from. To be a hit there was important of course. But you had to be a bigger hit on the rest of the circuit to get to the Palace. Bragging that you were a hit at the Palace only impressed small timers and hinterland theatres, where the manager could bill you as "Direct from the Palace, New York."

Actually, it was easy to be a hit at the Palace. The bigger triumph was in booking it. The only prestige playing there was to outsiders and not to the bookers. They had more respect for you if you were a hit at the Colonial, New York—Orpheum, Kansas City and Washington, D. C. Yet, if you flopped at the Palace, you did yourself immeasurable harm with these same bookers.

For some acts, the mere mention of the Palace was portentous. Some of the best names and big successes of vaudeville would not play there.

Some of them finally got the courage to accept the date, then suddenly fell ill, the day, or week before. I know of a few acts that got as far as showing up for orchestra rehearsal and then ran like hell out of the theatre, when they heard the overture.

There are those who played there who didn't care whether they interested the bookers or not. They wanted a Broadway show. There were acts that came from Broadway shows to play the Palace, only to impress show producers that they were star material.

The legitimate actors wanted this booking for the sole purpose of getting a year's route, because one year in vaudeville meant more money than five years in the legit.

The person wanting a Palace booking even more than the act was the agent. The reasons were: He could get the act a route (and maybe a raise) with nothing to do for a year but collect commissions. Added to this—prestige. He had the hit at the Palace! The actor would advertise, using his name, and gave him added respect with the bookers for his other acts, meaning more actors working, and fabulous commissions.

There were other kinds of agents too. They would react exactly as the guy above, but they gave you some thought while you were on the road. They'd read the reports and tip you off to criticisms—send suggestions and ideas, and keep your name alive in New York with publicity.

Maybe this is you, or someone you know. They were a small time act. "Oh, if we could only play the Palace, we'd show 'em," they said.

They did a good act and knew it. In fact, everyone knew it, except the guy who did the booking. He had caught them a couple of times, but he thought they just weren't right.

He didn't elucidate either. Usually this guy says, "They're not classy enough, they dress poorly, or, the material isn't for Broadway."

The girl in this act would do anything and did to play the Palace, but nobody knew it, except the girl and a flock of bookers. If you told this to the man in the act, he'd never believe it. Didn't he have a helluva act?

Then he got a great idea. They moved from the Somerset Hotel to the Astor. He rented a Rolls Royce for twenty bucks a day and drove it around and around the Palace building when the bookers went to lunch and in the evening when they were leaving for the day.

Three days and ninety dollars later, sure enough they were booked into the Palace. And to this day, this guy thinks it was the move to the Astor and the Rolls Royce that did the trick. And why shouldn't I?

38

============

One time we were booked on the Inter-State Circuit and were
sent to Wichita Falls, Texas, on our opening date. We arrived a day
ahead of time and went over to the theatre to see the manager.
The first thing he said was, "How do you make up?"

Figuring that he thought I was lazy about it, I assured him
that I used a full grease paint makeup.

"White face?" he asked sternly. I nodded.

"Then you'll have to blacken your face or not open at all," he
said. I tried to explain that my material wouldn't fit a blackface
character.

"Then," he said with finality, "you don't open. The Ku
Klux Klan is on the rampage and brother, you don't look like an
Egyptian!"

I wired Bob O'Donnell, head of the circuit, and he took a
plane from Fort Worth to Wichita Falls. His coming didn't solve
the situation—he was a Catholic. So I said, "There's only one
thing to do when the battle seems lost. Either charge or retreat."

"I get it," said Bob. "We'll attack."

That evening we loaded a small piano onto a cart and took it
to the hall where the hooded men were meeting. I rapped on the
door and eyes appeared in the slot. I told the guy we were the
vaudeville show from the Majestic Theatre. Would he and his
friends like some entertainment? He said to wait a minute, and
disappeared.

In a moment he was back and announced, "Go around to the
back." We did and unloaded the piano, pushing it into the hall. I
then walked front and center and stood for a moment modeling
my features, front view and profile, so all could see. Then I
shouted, "Brothers!"

They started to snicker and broke into a tremendous roar of
laughter. The ice was broken. I told them frankly why I had
come. Then I introduced Bob and announced, "Incidentally,
gentlemen, he is a Catholic." They took this good-naturedly also,
and so we started a show. It went over big.

The next day the theatre opening was a big success and we
did a record-breaking business throughout the circuit. The KKK
had passed the word along that we were all right. And this went

for the other members of the show who "didn't look exactly Egyptian" either.

I learned quickly a vaudevillian's total recall. That was to remember every act on an eight-act bill—when you were a hit—but have no recollection of even playing the theatre where I laid an egg.

I lied about my salary and came to believe my own lie, until I went to the bank.

We evaluated our contemporaries from the way they spoke. If you managed a sentence without an epithet, you were "putting on the dog." If your English was grammatically correct, you were "Joe College." If your manners were above reproach, you were a "fag." If you spoke exactly as we did, you were a bum.

The lesson that sent me running to buy a dictionary came about like this. While playing on the showboat, I shared a cabin (and dressing room) with an old guy about thirty. After being told no by that dame in cabin five, I came into the dressing room and politely screamed my head off about someone stealing my wardrobe. (B. S. Pulley and Lenny Bruce would have loved my rhetoric.) My roommate gave me the "Joe College" with, "Since you talk like a toilet, you will dress in there." That was more than fifty years ago. You should have as many good years ducking taxes as dictionaries I've worn out.

We learned that it paid to advertise, long before that guy came up with gimmick "tired blood."

Typical ads of the day were:

Juvenile	Sing (and/or) dance. Have tux will travel. Send ticket.
Female	Classical or popular singer, have three changes of gowns and orchestrations. Won't mix. Send railroad fare.
Comic	Original jokes, no Joe Millers. Send ticket.

Acrobats didn't have to advertise, they were always in demand.

The firsthand balancing team I ever worked with made this classic observation. While doing a head to head balance, the top mounter noticed a well-dressed man in the first row not applauding. He sotto voce'd to the grunting bottom man, "I bet he ain't got brains enough to do a handstand."

In nineteen seventeen, I played on the bill with the Marx Brothers and Mother Minnie in Muncie, Indiana. I became acquainted with Zeppo and asked if Harpo was deaf and dumb. He told me this. His uncle, Al Shean (of Gallagher and Shean fame) wrote the act and forgot to write lines for Harpo. What Harpo did came out of his beautiful mind.

While putting this down, I had to go to the sandbox, which caused me to be grateful that it was right in the confines of my living quarters. Man, how many times did I run down to the only privy on my floor in a flea bag hotel, or rooming house? I still hear that stentorian voice coming from within saying, "Be out in a minute."

In my second week with a burlesque show I met Jack Dempsey in Memphis. He was with the "Sells Floto" circus meeting all comers. I knew Jack Kearns who invited me to play pinochle with Dempsey and a couple of his guys. (Not Teddy Hayes and Jerry, his trainers, they came a bit later.)

The first time I saw Dempsey he was bare from the waist up. If a man's body can be beautiful, his was. Then came a high pitched voice that didn't match the body at all and it shocked the hell out of me.

Jack left the room to take a couple of aspirins. Kearns handed me a little box and said quickly, "Tell him these are the best things in the world for a headache." I didn't have time to ask why, as I heard Jack's voice sing "Who's deal is it?"

I did ask Dempsey about the headaches and he explained the reason. He would take on five or six bruisers a day and accidentally these guys would sneak in a punch, or clumsily bump heads with him.

It wasn't until after he beat Jess Willard for the championship that I found out what was in that little box.

Dempsey was playing the Pantages time, while I was touring the Orpheum circuit. Strangely enough, it was in Memphis again. He was doing three shows a day, while I was doing two. So between shows I'd visit with him. By this time, Teddy Hayes and Jerry (can't think of his name) was with him; also Freddy Behrens, his orchestra leader.

He gave me a big hello, spun me around and slapped my fanny so hard his fingerprints were on me for a week. "What the hell is that for?" I bellowed. Imitating a sissy, he said, "For the saltpeter tablets you gave me for a headache."

I'll never forget the veins in the manager's forehead sticking out a foot, when he brought Dempsey's salary to Kearns.

You've got to feel for the managers in the early vaudeville days. Here was a guy getting thirty five bucks a week and paying hundreds and thousands to actors who had a hell of a time counting up to ten. (The figure ten we knew because that was the commission we paid.)

So you can imagine how he felt laying those bundles of bills in front of Kearns. Apropos of salaries—at a time when I was getting a hundred and a quarter a week the opening and closing acts were getting about sixty two fifty. Other acts on the bill got two fifty, five hundred and a headliner like Paul Whiteman thirty five hundred.

Some of us big timers would ignore the opening and closing acts. However, came July first, those poor dumb acts would knock off until September. They would pack up their lousy Cadillacs and LaSalles, drive to some crumby lake, where they had some kind of a cottage that slept six, and a kakamamie boat that only slept four.

But we, the ignorers, were looking for the "last half" someplace, or living off our relatives.

The same shtoonks that ignored the dumb acts, gave the brush to stagehands too. They'd yell at them, "Hey, you!"

After the matinee you went to some joint where they reheated yesterday's soup and poured hot gravy over yesterday's roast beef. But "hey, you," got into his car, drove to his lovely home in the suburbs and had a meal cooked that evening.

You didn't brush the orchestra leader. Oh no! He could make or break you with one swish of his baton, (usually a fiddle bow).

Oh yes, there were some who saved their money. I want to tell you of one guy who didn't and it cost him.

Joe Frisco was offered twenty five hundred a week, but held out for thirty five hundred. During that time, he had a little trouble paying his bills. He was brought to his senses by Solly

42

Violinsky. (I'll tell you about him in a minute.)

Solly gave Frisco some sage advice, by asking him, "Joe, how does it feel to lay off at a big salary?" Frisco went back to work. Violinsky was a concert violinist and pianist. A solid headliner with a great sense of humor, offstage. His funny cracks would come at you like he was spitting bullets, but he never in all his lifetime made a funny at somebody else's expense. There was none of that, "You're so fat that . . . or she's so skinny that . . . or he's so cheap that . . ." Here are a couple of examples of his humor.

A bunch of us from the Friars Club went to Sing Sing Prison to do a show. Solly misjudged a step, fell to the concrete and broke his arm. The first people to get to him were Bobby Clark and Harry Hershfield. Bobby tearfully asked, "Solly, are you hurt badly?" He answered, "I've been waiting a whole year for a break and I finally got it," then passed out.

Later in the Prison hospital, someone asked him if he was insured. He said, "Yes, for fire and theft."

The next morning in the Princeton Hotel (we were both living there; my room was next door to a suite he occupied with Benny Ryan and Bert Hanlon), I asked if I could shave him. He answered, "No, if it's good enough for Lincoln, it's good enough for me."

Ryan and Hanlon were both vaudevillians and songwriters. They wrote the lyrics to a lot of Solly's melodies.

Bert joined the Navy. Benny tried but was rejected. Solly was turned down because of age. Seriously he said, "How can a guy be too old to lead a band?" Bert said, "You're too old to march." Solly answered, "I wouldn't have to march if that band was on a ship, would I?" Benny asked, "Don't you know that while everybody was getting off in lifeboats, you and your band would be on the top deck playing "Nearer My God to Thee?" Solly answered, "My band would be so well rehearsed, they could play it without me."

While on the subject of fast answers, this one comes to mind. In Philadelphia there were two agents by the names of Sablosky and McGurk.

Since you couldn't work in Pennsylvania on Sunday, Sablosky and McGurk took up the slack in your bankroll by booking you in Camden, New Jersey. (In Pittsburgh you played Steubenville,

Ohio on Sunday.) On one of those occasions, Sablosky called to offer me Camden, but at a deep cut in salary. Very politely I screamed at him, "Why?" He reminded me that it was Holy Week. (Holy Week and Christmas week were the worst at the box office.)

I asked, "What has Holy Week got to do with you?"

He answered, "I'm speaking for McGurk."

Camden reminded me of a guy, I'll call Little Sir Ego. On that same bill was a female impersonator, who was such a hit as a girl he didn't have to remove the wig at the finish of his act to prove he was clever. Mr. Ego had never seen him before and went on the make for him.

He asked the impersonator to have night lunch with him and the invitation was accepted. When the guy showed up in male garb, Ego went along with the gag and wound up with a shiner bluer than Jack Benny's eyes.

Even if some of us couldn't spell cat and wore suspenders and a belt, we had ethics. We never told a joke about cripples, spastics, stutterers or hunchbacks. The word cockeyes was verboten even in a drink joke. While telling jokes or playing a scene we never yelled FIRE. This could cause a stampede, where people could be trampled. Yawning was out too; it could be contagious and you'd blow your audience. It was an unwritten law that no matter how big a hit you were, you did not "milk" the audience for applause. You took two bows and did an encore. Sketches took no more than five curtain calls and made a "thank you" speech.

The smart performer never stopped the show, he helped keep it going!

Oh yes, there were pigs that had tricks to keep the applause going and some acts didn't know when to get off. We called them "Chinese" acts, Ontoolong and Bowtoolong. Goodman Ace (when he was a critic on the Kansas City *Star*) said of an act, "They went on second and came off next to closing."

Before they had MC's acts were announced by Enunciators on either side of the stage. The considerate MC never told a joke ahead of a comedy act. In my day you never heard an MC ask the audience to applaud the entrance of an act, nor did he ask the audience to applaud at the finish of an act.

You see, the correct way of presenting an act, by Bob Hope,

44

who will announce the name, then say "right here." Jack Benny is also a good example. He will announce the act, face them, and either exit when the applause subsides, or give them his full attention until they speak. When that act exits, Jack will again show them respect by facing them when they go off, and again, never speak until the applause stops. He usually says, "Wasn't he, or she marvelous?"

Danny Thomas does a nice thing too. He'll start the applause and face the entrance the act is coming from, but never ask you to applaud. His end remark is usually: "Don't you love him?" (or her, or them) Wonderful, just wonderful."

Hey, I got ahead of myself! Let's go back to my era.

I wish you could have been there when, during the first world war, to hear the German acrobats cop out, that were not Teutons.

One acrobat continually yodeled and declared himself a Swiss. Another guy waited until all the acts were onstage, waiting to rehearse their music and burst through the stagedoor yelling, "Doorman, do you got zumm mail for de Patr-r-riks?"

============

Here is a sample of the bits (now called SHTIK) that we did in a tab show in nineteen fourteen.

(Dutch)	Gooten morgen, Patrick.
(Irish)	And a how de do to you Shultz. Lovely day to be here in the park, ain't it?
(Dutch)	It's a nize day awright, too bad you ain't here.
(Irish)	What do you mean I'm not here? Are you dafft?
(Dutch)	Look, I don't want no trouble mit you, but I bet you mit ten dollars what you ain't here.
(Irish)	Well, I never heard of such a thing.
(Dutch)	There's my ten dollars, would you like to make mit a wager?
(Irish)	No sooner said then done, here's me ten dollars, now. . . .

(Dutch)	I like to ask you zomding. You ain't in Philamdelphia, is you?
(Irish)	Of course not.
(Dutch)	And you couldn't be in Zinsanapolis is you?
(Irish)	No, I ain't in Philadelphia and I ain't in Cincinnati.
(Dutch)	Well, if you ain't in Philamdelphia and you didn't wass in Zinsanapolis, you must be zomeplace else. Right?
(Irish)	That's correct.
(Dutch)	Zo, if you're someplace *else* you couldn't be here. I took money, auf weidersein!
(Irish)	Well, I'll be a monkey's uncle. Bad 'cess to you, you. . . . Well, hello there, Sinzberg.
(Jewish)	Hello, Patrick.
(Irish)	I'll bet you're glad to be here, ain't ya?
(Jewish)	I'm glad to be alive.
(Irish)	I'll bet you ten dollars.
(Jewish)	Here's my ten dollars.
(Irish)	Now, then, you ain't in Pennselvania are you?
(Jewish)	What are you talking about?
(Irish)	Well, you bet ten dollars.
(Jewish)	On what did I betting?
(Irish)	Oh, I forgot to tell you, I'm betting you ten dollars you ain't here.
(Jewish)	This is some kind of a crazy?
(Irish)	I'm bettin ya ten dollars you *ain't*.
(Jewish)	You could make it twenny, if this is your perogatee.
(Irish)	All right twenty it is. Now then, you ain't in Peiensilvania, are

	you?
(Jewish)	Not this season.
(Irish)	You ain't in Alabamee. . . .
(Jewish)	You could bet fifty on this.
(Irish)	Well, if you ain't in Peinsilvania, or Alabammee, you must be some place else, and if you're someplace else you can't be here. . . .
(Jewish)	You got right.
(Irish)	Hey, wait, wait now, what are you takin the money for?
(Jewish)	Who took the money?
(Irish)	You did, I saw you with me own eyes.
(Jewish)	Hold you hosses. If I ain't in Peinsilwaynia and I ain't in Alabamee, I must be someplace else, ain't I? If I am someplace else, how could I take the money?
(Irish)	You dirty. . . .

============

One of the worst things that can happen to a vaudevillian happened to me. I laughted so hard at two acts ahead of me, I got so hoarse, I could barely do my own act.

I won't do Roger Imhoff's whole act, just his opening, it killed me.

He was a vegetable farmer who had had an accident and couldn't get a room in the only hotel in town.

With his throaty, guttural flannel-mouth Irish, he said to the clerk, "If there ever was a man who had hard luck, tis I. Here I am forty miles away from home, with a load of vegetables and a dead horse on me hands. I walked all the way here and I got corns, with bunions on top of them."

============

Alan Cross and Henry Dunn (nee Abie Grossman and Henry

Levine) were considered on a par with Van and Schenk, the finest singing duo in vaudeville.

When two shows a day big time vaudeville died and the three a day small time degenerated into four and five a day nightmares, the classy Alan Cross retired. He opened a delicatessen in (I think) Providence, Rhode Island, which flourished.

The large sized and big hearted Henry Dunn would never work with another partner and decided to do a single.

He bought a few jokes, remembered a couple more and broke his act in around Boston. Naturally, he was a smash hit with his singing but Henry was not too good a joke teller. On the advice of his agent, he came to New York and sought out one of the best comedy writers around. Jackie Barnett, who still is one of the heavyweights in the comedy field. The agent booked Henry in a little theatre in Brooklyn, so Jackie could see what Henry did, and advise him.

He stood in the entrance and heard that magnificent voice thrill the people and then fall on his can with the jokes.

Henry finished to great applause and exuberantly asked, "Well, what do you think, Jackie?"

Jackie's reply was, "The wrong guy opened the delicatessen."

============

Here's one that's even older than Jack Benny.

A lady came to a photographer and said, "Meester, mine husband is expiring and the only *thing* what I got left to remembering him is this tintype."

He said, "That little picture is quite an antique. What can I do for you?"

She said, "I don't like the way he sitting with one eye closed. Could you open the eye?"

The man said he thought he could.

She continued, "And that cap what he's wearing is a stinky. Could you take off this terrible thing?"

The man said, "Yes, I can remove the cap, but you'll have to tell me *how* he parted his hair."

She said, "What's got to do the parting?"

He said, "I'll have to know if he combed his hair straight

back and if he *did* part it, on what side was the part?"

She said, "You scientix is so smart, but also you're dumb. When you'll take off the hat, wouldn't you'll see?"

============

The loveable Lebanese knows about this, so don't think I'm discrediting Danny Thomas. Of course, you've screamed at him telling his famous Jack story; I know I have.

In 1917 I heard Bucky Carleton tell it this way.

As Pat opened the door, Molly said to him:

SHE:	It's about time you got home, we're going to be late for Clancy's funeral.
HIM:	Wait now. Hush. We'll not be goin to Clancy's funeral. It's not fit for man nor beast to be out in that blindin snow. The street cars are not runnin and there's no way for us to get to the Simmiterry.
SHE:	Why don't you go over to Murphy's and ask him for the loan of his horse and sleigh? He's bedridden with Penomonie and he can't leave the house.
HIM:	I'll not go over embarrass meself by him telling me no.
SHE:	There you are jumpin off the cliff before you're pushed. You have not asked him yet and you're already having him tell you no. Whoash go now!
HIM:	All right, I'll go, but I *know* he won't give it to me.

On his way to Murphy's house, he was talking to himself, and getting angrier with every thought.

I'll ask him for the loan of his horse and sleigh and if he says no, I'll offer to pay the rent of it. If he says no to that, I'll offer to *feed* the *horse.* If the louse refuses that, I'll offer to buy the *horse,* I'll buy the *sleigh* I'll. . . .

By that time he was in front of Murphy's house. He rang the bell and when Murphy weakly opened the door and politely asked, "What can I do for you, Patsy?" Clancy yelled, "You can take your horse and sleigh and. . . .

============

Before Fred Allen left us to make the angels laugh, we used to kid about a routine a couple of guys did in 1910. It went something like this. Hey, Henry, I see you got money; is you been working?

Yes, sir, I got me a wonderful job, I got a thousand people under me.

A thousand people under you? Boy what kind a job you got?

I'm a night watchman in a semmetree.

A semmettree, what's that?

You know anything about golf.

Yeh.

Well, that's the *last* hole. I sittin in that semmettree the other night and a big white skilleken walk up behind me. He say to me, boy how'd you get out this here place?

My feet looked at me and I looked at them and man we understood each other. I said to that skilleken, *follow me.* Then I started runnin. I run so fast, my vest pocket was dippin sand. I turned the corner into a fence—there was no corner *there,* so I *made* one. They was a farmer who thot I was bergeler and he shot at me. I heard that bullet when it passed *me* and I heard it again when I passed *it.*

After I run about five miles I sat down on a log to rest. Who come sit beside me? The skilleken. He said, boy, we run some, didn't we?

I said yes sir and we gonna run some mo. And I was gone!

============

In my first year on the big time in nineteen twenty, my name was not up in lights, nor did it appear on the marquees, but it was on the posters (called three sheets) outside of the theatre. You would have had a hard time finding it unless you were a dog.

So to get my name more familiar with the bookers and newspaper people, I had these booklets printed.

============

They are over here . . .

Very little of the contents was original with me. I culled jokes and—so-called—wisecracks from two old joke books, i. e. Joe Miller and Madison's Budget.

Appearing on a TV show recently I heard a new young comic tell the assistant producer what he wanted the emcee to say in his introduction. The emcee said it.

"Ladies and Gentlemen, here is Sam Tranafats, a new young comedian who is refreshing in that he writes his own material."

The following is the material he said he wrote that came out of my booklets and I purloined from Miller and Madison.

"Hello Folks. I just saw in the papers that a man who spoke ten languages married a lady who spoke five. I'll bet on the lady."

"Ladies and Gentlemen, we have a celebrity in the house, Sonny Liston. (We used to say Strangler Lewis.) Oh, I'm sorry, you look just like him. Pardon me Lady."

In the early twenties I asked Walter Winchell to give me a plug and he did by printing the following joke. He was honest enough to say, it was an oldie.

"A tired actor said to a Pullman agent, I want a berth in the sleeper. The agent asked, upper or lower. The actor asked what's the difference? The Pullman agent said, 20%, the lower is higher than the upper. The higher price is for the lower. If you want the lower, you'll have to go higher, etc., etc., etc."

Now then, I know the cliche, "A joke is new if you haven't heard it." It just bugged me to hear the guy say he wrote it. The topper is the audience laughed at the stuff and in the following interview, the emcee sincerely asked, "How do you think up such funny stuff?"

The comic casually replied, "Just from the true happenings I see every day."

For the guy's sake, I hope Winchell didn't see him.

SIGNS OF THE TIMES

Many theatres displayed these signs backstage:

Don't send your laundry out until after the second show. Don't tell us what you did at Palace, do it here. Do not use the words hell, damn, hunchback, or cockeyed. No cooking, or sleeping in dressing rooms.

In theatres in the South: Do not make mention of the KKK in any manner.

In Boston: If you use the word pants in your act, change it to trousers. No dancing allowed on Sundays. If you move around while singing do not walk in tempo with the music.

In Pittsburgh: No drawing on salary until after the third day. Reference to ladies undergarments, will result in immediate cancellation.

In Lincoln, Nebraska: Please eliminate all references to farmers as Rubes.

In Wichita Falls, Texas: Please do not use hell, damn, or make reference to a dog's gender.

In Forth Worth, Texas: Do not refer to John Nance Garner's middle name in jest.

I never did find out if this was a gag or not, but one place (in upstate New York) had this sign: Please do not flush the toilet while the sketch is on.

All trains displayed this sign: Do not flush toilets while standing in the depot.

Every vaudevillian could sing this; see if you can. It's to the melody of "Humoresque":

Customers will please refrain

From flushing toilets, while the train,
Is standing in the station, I love you.

RECIPE FOR REVENGE

I'll lay you twenty to one that you never heard of this rib, unless you knew the shtoonks who were the "patsies."

Number one stinker was a producer in on a rain check. Nepotism. This guy like to broke the studio with his bad judgment.

He invited a bunch of people to a party he was giving in honor of having one of his pictures almost break even. Who did he invite? Natch, some guys just like him, otherwise I'd have never pulled such a gag. The tip-off on what kind of a guy I am, he invited me too.

To get even for the little people these guys kicked around, I got some of those capsules that produced colors when one relieves oneself.

At strategic moments, I mixed the brown ingredients with the chopped liver, red with the beets, green with the onion dip, yellow with the deviled eggs and blue with the caviar in the hors d'oeuvres.

To wait for somewhere over the rainbow is murder. You find yourself laughing at someone breaking a leg skiing and a guy going into bankruptcy.

From left field you are helping the bartender serve, you pick up half-filled glasses and you become the hostess' little helper, by continually passing the hors d'oeuvres.

Who had to go first? Henry the host. He used the guest powder room rather than the one in the master bedroom. He wasn't in there a minute, till we heard him yell, "Clara, come in here!!!" Clara was singing her head off at the piano, but didn't answer till she came to the end of a phrase.

"Whatta want?"

"Will you please come in here?"

"I swear that man will drive me crazy." No sooner than she entered the bathroom, "You dirty rotten . . ."

"Clara, I swear by my mother I didn't do nothin."

We didn't hear any more until she dialed the phone to her doctor. The singers at the piano all cued each other at the same time, and what were they belting, but singing in the rain. Their heads didn't move much, but all did a pan shot with their eyes on Henry as he hurried to his bedroom.

A couple of minutes later we heard another clarion call from the privy.

"Zelda, come in here!"

"What the hell is this, did he get his zipper caught too?"

"ZELDA!!!"

"Yeh, yeh, I'm coming." She disappears.

"Oh, my Gawd! You dirty, stinkin, lousy son of a . . ."

"Zelda, I swear by my mother . . ."

"You swear, you swear, you all swear by your mother, did you give *me* one thought and how about the children?"

We hear no more and the room begins to buzz. In a couple of minutes, they go to the closet for their clothes. They don't speak and nobody dares to ask. As they are leaving, in comes a doctor. Zelda stops. "Doc, you better take a look at this louse, too." Her husband follows the doc.

I turn to a lady I know and confess to the gag, it hits her so funny, she runs for the bathroom. The singing starts again and stops again, when we hear a shriek from the bathroom. "Jesse, come in here!" Jesse runs like hell to his wife. We hear no dialogue.

From the bedroom comes the doctor and two relieved husbands laughing hysterically. The doctor explains the gag and everybody hollers their heads off. The lady comes out of the bathroom—"Oscar, play the song that fits this occasion, 'Over the Rainbow'."

Before they can get started, Henry announces, "There's only one way to find out who the Rembrandt is. As custodian of the can, all male members will pass before me in review." After a

couple of guys go in, I sneak out the back entrance. I wasn't a
very colorful guy anyway.

MARXISMS

A gang of us was sitting around not enjoying each other's company. There were too many comics holding our breaths until the other too funny comic told his favorite joke.

It was at Zeppo Marx's house, right after the mad Marxes invaded Hollywood. Chico, Groucho, Harpo and Gummo were surrounded by Cantor, Jessel, Jesse Block, Eve Sully, Al Boasberg and me.

Someone started to relate funny practical jokes. One in particular hit Groucho as the funniest. So Al Boasberg said, "I know a guy I'd like to pull this on." He dialed Groucho's number and talked to Arthur Sheekman who was living with Groucho. (Natch, Groucho didn't know it was happening to him, so he laughed his funny head off.)

Boasberg very officially told Sheekman that he was with the Beverly Hills Water Department and that there was a break in the main water line. He said that it would take a couple of hours to fix and advised Sheekman to fill every available vessel in the house with water, so he'd have drinking and bathing water for the morning.

When Groucho arrived home, he saw bowls of water all over the place. The washbowls in five bathrooms were filled, as were the bathtubs, and every pot and pan in the kitchen sparkled with water.

He didn't tip his mitt to Sheekman that he had been had, but when Arthur went to his room, he emptied the pots and pans and pulled the plugs in the bathrooms. He looked into the mirror and said, "Remind me tomorrow to have Zeppo punch Boasberg on the

============

I won't tell you this fellow's name, because he's still around and I don't want his kids laughing at him.

He laughed his head off at practical jokes, especially when they were his. Then to my amazement he said, "Anyone that would go for those gags is a moron." That hurt the stinker in me and this is what I done did.

His automobile license was in my view every day, because I parked near him at the studio. Zeppo Marx, who matches my stinkiness to the letter had a gang of us at his house for dinner and everyone was in on the gag.

I Irish-brogued him into believing I was a sergeant of the police on the phone. He answered yes to the make of car he owned, the color and the license plate. I told him that we had his car at the station. We had recovered it after it was either stolen or taken for a ride by some kids. He said he'd be right down to pick it up.

All of us ran over to his house (around the corner from Zeppo) and saw him get into the very car he was going to the police station to recover. He hadn't gone more than a couple of blocks before he realized what had happened to him. Screech went the brakes, he made a U-turn to get back to his house, and there, sitting on his lawn, were all of us who heard him make the crack about the moron.

To prove he was a good sport, he invited the gang in for a drink. If you read this any place else you wouldn't believe it, but when he walked us outside to say goodnight, his car had really been stolen.

============

The great theatrical critic, Alexander Woolcott, lived in the Algonquin Hotel in New York. His most beloved possession was a little dog. Harpo Marx, one of his closest friends, knew that when he was reviewing a play, Mr. Woolcott would go to a phone at intermission and call the hotel. The operator would ring his room three times.

On one such occasion, Harpo duked a bellhop a fin to passkey him into Mr. Woolcott's room. When the phone rang, Harpo lifted the receiver off the cradle and barked joyously into the phone.

No one ever tipped him to the gag and he's probably still bragging about it to Burns Mantle, Ashton Stevens and George Jean Nathan, up there in Shubert's Alley in the sky.

=============

Harpo had a crazy looking golf cap that made him look like a gangster. That was enough reason for him to buy a couple of dollars worth of jewelry at Woolworth's.

He walked into Tiffany's, turned and stood immediately by the door. When he saw what was the most foot traffic, he bounced out of the door, tripped and let the phony jewelry scatter to the sidewalk, and ran.

You conjure up the picture in your own mind, of dozens of sedate and so-called legitimate people on their hands and knees fighting for the loot.

=============

"There's one in every crowd," has a different connotation here. He didn't own the act, he wasn't the star, nor was he the manager. Yet, without him handling the many details that go with a troupe's success, they'd be in a lot of trouble.

Such a guy was Jack Crandell who was with Eddie Cantor for years. At this particular time, he carried the burden of the Cantor-Jessel traveling vaudeville show. The big mystery about Jack was, when did he find time to sleep?

It was about eleven o'clock closing night in Buffalo. He announced to Eddie and George, "I'm going down to check the sleeping car, and if everything is okay, I'll turn in. See you tomorrow morning in New York."

About a quarter of twelve the gang hopped into their compartments and lower berths. Eddie and George had drawing room A. They took a gander at Jack snoring melodiously in lower seven.

Both of them stripped to the waist and waited for the train to pull out. As soon as it got rolling, Jessel put some shaving cream on half of his face and with razor in hand, woke Crandell with, "Come on, Jack, we'll be in in about fifteen minutes!" Jack looked at George through half closed eyes and saw the shaving cream. "Boy, I must have slept like a dead man."

He crawled out of his lower, looked into the drawing room and saw Cantor with a towel over his face. "I felt like I only just now went to sleep." He hurried to the men's washroom. What he thought was Cantor wiping his face was actually Cantor laughing so hard his choppers flew into the towel.

In the washroom he got into a beef with the porter about his watch being wrong. Crandell was no whispering Jack Smith and the noise brought yells from the troupe to hold it down.

When Jack realized he had been had, he apologized to the porter and went back to bed.

He rose early and sneaked off the train at a hundred and twenty fifth street. You never saw more confusion in a two-reeler than what happened when the troupe arose. All of their shoes were jumbled into a mass, under the mattress in lower seven. Cantor's and Jessel's were on the bottom with the laces knotted.

What was it that was making the porter bite his lip to keep him from laughing? That beautiful ten dollar bill in his pocket that Jack had given him.

============

THE PLACE: Jake Adler's Frolics Cafe on the south side of Chicago.

THE TIME: Early Twenties.

A small combo played for dancing and a ragtime piano player played for the entertainers.

The comic did his routines in one spot. The singers sang a verse and chorus center stage, then moved from table to table. This was called "busking." The customer tipped them according to his standing in the community.

The customers were ninety nine percent the mob. The one percent were privileged people, like theatrical performers or politicians.

Look over there to where Al Capone is sitting at the head of a long table. His guests are Johnny Torrio, Dinney Cooney, Ralph Gilless, Bud Gentry, his brothers Ralph, Mimi and their ladies. You can't see it, but the wall panels behind big Al are plates of steel. You see, there were some naughty boys from the North side who wished to do him harm.

This particular night was tense with excitement. Gun play or police interference was not expected, but honoring them with his presence, was to be, one Gene Buck.

Mr. Buck represented Florenz Ziegfeld and was coming there to see their favorite singer (at the time), Cliff Edwards. You may have known him as "Ukelele Ike," Edwards of Clayton and Edwards, or the comic in many movies. If you're too old for that, shake hands with the guy who is "Jimminy Cricket" for Walt Disney.

This digression is important. They had another favorite, a waiter. His name was Louis Josephs, a boxer who had seen better days. They loved him for his congeniality and trigger wit.

When Gene Buck arrived with W. C. Fields, Dave Stamper and Edna Leedom, it was about a half hour before show time. The waiter borrowed somebody's fancy derby from the checkroom, snatched a dollar cigar from Capone's table, and started to shadow box on the floor. The band followed his moves by playing "Strutters Ball." His nimble footwork to music created a new kind of dance and his juggling of a lighted cigar intrigued Fields.

Yes, Gene Buck signed him and used his nickname, Joe Frisco. Of course, Cliff Edwards was his usual hit and he too got a contract.

The only person I know who was there that fateful night is the man they call the beloved gentleman of the Lambs Club. His name is Jack Waldron. He didn't get a contract from Gene Buck, but the one the "boys" gave him wasn't bad either. "You're here for the rest of your life, and if the joint burns down, we'll build you a club of your own."

The best way I can describe Waldron is, he was the first Don Rickles and Jack E. Leonard. His task was a little more difficult, however, because he insulted guys who would shoot you for saying 'are not' instead of 'ain't.'

============

Years ago, a comic I knew, had just concluded a fifty three week tour. But he only played thirty five out of the fifty three.

You don't have to be a performer to realize that those eighteen weeks of not working and living away from home can make you good and broke.

And on top of it, he gave himself the luxury of having his non-working wife traveling with him.

When he arrived in New York, his wife's father met them, and after the hugging and kissing, asked, "What do you got there in the box with the holes?"

His daughter said, "Oh, Pa, wait'll you see the cute little bull-dog Joe brought me. You'll love him."

Pa said, "I don't need no bulldogs to dirty up mine apartment. Well, anyway, I thought what I'll tell you. I'm making a party tonight; my friends and the neighbors should meet mine son-in-law the big actor."

Joe thanked him for his thoughtfulness, then Pa said, "Fifty three weeks, huh? My, my! I'll bet you saved up a bundle money."

Joe said, "No, Pa, between the layoffs, commission and expenses, we barely had enough money to come home."

Pa said, "Is that's all? You're in a nice business, wodervill."

That night at the party, Pa called everyone to attention and said, "Every people, I want you should meet mine son-in-law, what he's a big actor from the wodervill. He's killing the people in pieces and he's making them fall down from laughing. He just now is playing fifty three weeks, and he saved up a bulldog."

============

This one was really a kick in the head.

Sime Silverman who founded the "Theatrical Bible"—*Variety*, was also a working variety mug. He didn't like an act because of their risque material and said so in his review. The male member of the team said, "I'm goin right over to the *Variety* and punch that guy on the nose."

Next day I asked, "Did you punch Sime on the nose?" He answered, "Nah, it's a dame—her real name is Simone."

============

You had to be there to see the look on the face of the manager of Fox Cretona Theatre.

Jim Barton, the most versatile actor that ever trod the boards had it in his contract that his name alone appear on all three sides of the marquee. It was there all right, but above his name (on all three sides) was the title of the movie, *Seventh Heaven.*

Jim sent for the manager and told him to remove the picture billing. After some bickering, the manager exploded, "Do you want me to take Mr. Fox's name down too?" Jim quietly answered, "No, leave it up there, just don't light it."

============

This is one of those unbelievables, but it's true. My agent, Max Hayes, went to a doctor to see about recurring headaches. After a long examination, the doctor advised, "Your troubles will be over if you have your teeth extracted." Max extracted his uppers and lowers and asked, "Do you mean these?"

============

I was on the bill with a "mind-reading" act that Max handled. This lady thrilled and confounded audiences (me too) with her revelations. One day I innocently asked her, "Where do you go next week?" She snapped at me, "How the hell do I know until I hear from Max?"

This same lady's husband did a "protean" act. His lightning changes of clothing were amazing. Every article of clothing was in perfect detail, but invariably he left the theatre with his fly open.

THE ORPHEUM CIRCUIT

Max Hayes got me the Orpheum circuit. While at the Orpheum in Los Angeles, my wife declared she didn't ever want to see the East or its cold winters again. Couldn't I either get into pictures or find some work out here?

I went to Fanchon and Marco and offered to cut my salary to MC for them, as Gene Morgan and Rube Wolf were doing. They liked the idea; I would be a good name for them and the cut salary was perfect for their budget. However, to MC these shows you also had to be a bandleader. I told them I'd be glad to, but they explained that to lead a band, one must join the Musicians Union.

"Okay, I'll join," I said. "Call the guy from the union and I'll pay him the dues."

But it wasn't done just that way. You had to go to union headquarters with your instrument and qualify. To me, this is nothing—I borrow a trombone and go to the union. Three guys greet me like six dead fish-eyes. They put a sheet of music on a rack and tell me to play the thing. This is no time to explain that they didn't teach me to read music in the reform school.

I say, "Look, gentlemen, do you want something fast or slow? This thing you want me to play is kid stuff."

One man replies, "Play both slow and fast."

You'd be surprised, but I get a pretty nice tone out of the trombone and they okay me!

I ran to the phone, called my wife at the Biltmore Hotel and said, "Kid, we're in! Go find a house to buy or rent." I don't think she waited for the elevator to get to the street. By that afternoon we had rented a house in Hollywood.

Opening matinees at Loew's State I conducted that band with such ferocity that I wore myself out before half the show was over. I waved the baton in march style when the boys were playing a soft, sweet, Hawaiian waltz. Since the jokes and dancing were good, nobody cared too much.

Fanchon and Marco came back with two strange guys. They complimented me on the show and were going to have their lawyer draw up a contract. The two guys were the pianist Ernie Wehl, and the first violinist, Julius. Fan and Mike had decided that from now on I need not wave the baton madly, that Ernie would give me the fast tempos with his head at the piano, and Julius the slow ones with his violin. This was good. Most bandleaders would beat off a number and wave the baton while smiling at the audience. I got compliments for not doing that. Little did the customers realize that if I ever turned to them I was lost.

The next show was better. By the fourth one I was a full-fledged leader, and Marco was talking about making the contract for five years. That night at the Biltmore, my wife and I were happy with our future prospects. Tomorrow, while I was working, she'd move us into the new home.

Next day I went to the theatre full of joy, whistling and humming my way across the busy streets. The doorman was glad to see me and stagehands yelled their hellos. The musicians greeted me nicely, too. I hadn't acted like a "know-it-all" to them and asked, rather than told. It seemed funny that all that day and night I hadn't seen Fan or Mike. After the last show I went to the manager's office to draw some cash. There sat Fan, Mike, the manager and press agent. I thought the greeting wasn't exactly cool, but something was wrong. Fan and Mike weren't given to solemnity. "Say, what's wrong?" would have been the wrong approach with them, so I asked if I had hurt their feelings, or had done something wrong on the stage. Then Mike explained.

The feature writer and syndicated columnist on the *Examiner* had panned the life out of me. She was Louella O. Parsons, a power in the press and with the people. She could make your theatre or movie, or ruin you completely. After I read the notice, I said, "This is not true. She can't mean me; after she says I'm not a hit with the audience (which is a lie and you know it) she goes on to say, 'Why don't I stick to my fiddle?' "

Marco replied he knew I didn't play violin and certainly I was a hit with the audience, but nobody contradicts Parsons. The investment in the theatre was worth more than any comic, so he'd have to protect the theatre.

That was it. No contract, no work after closing night—and here I was with a lease on my hands. What would I tell my wife?

Closing night came and if you've ever been shown great love, then you'll appreciate the goodbyes of the chorus, musicians and stagehands. It was heartwarming. Sure, I'd been fired before, quit, been refused and even cancelled—but never before so unjustly. The ride home in the car was awful. Each block we sped past was just so much nearer to having to tell a happy girl the news I was carrying in my heart.

We arrived. I got a big hug and kiss, and I sat down at a table loaded with goodies. I started to explain the suitcase and my wife said, "I'm glad you brought your laundry home for me to do instead of taking it to those places that ruin it." I slowly told my tale. I don't remember sleeping that night.

The phone rang early the next morning. It was Marco. I was to go to Grauman's Egyptian Theatre where an act fell out.

I grabbed my suitcase, hung up a couple of suits and went onstage for music rehearsal. They wouldn't need me for an hour or more, I was told. Got talking to Lyda Roberti, a chorus girl who later became a star. She told me there were only three shows a day. Ho, ho, my tricky mind starts talking to me: This is only three shows a day against four and five at Loew's State. There are windows and fresh air in the dressing rooms, the reverse of the cellar in the State, and I'm only six or seven blocks from my house. I'll go find the manager and start pitching for a regular job.

He was sitting about in the middle of the house, watching the rehearsal. His name was Louis Edelman, now and for the last thirty five years a top producer in Hollywood. He is the man that gave Danny Thomas his big start in TV, and is one of the creators of "The Big Valley." I called his name and started my pitch. He cut me with, "You're Rubin, saw you at the Orpheum and State, and you're okay. Now listen, they don't go for comics in this house, but don't worry about it. I'll give you a good report anyway. See you later." There went my pitch, my little dream house tumbled.

You won't believe this, but right at that same moment, Lynn Cowan was singing a song he had written called "In a Little Dream House." I went backstage dejectedly and rehearsed my music half-heartedly.

I don't know why, or how it happened, but the audience was a pushover. They laughed in the right places and made an awful fool of Mr. Edelman's speech. I've always been a good hoofer, but not as good as that audience made me with their applause! The show over, Mr. Edelman came back immediately and explained that the following week was Lynn Cowan's last, and would I please stay over and put on some kind of act that would fit the situation? Would I stay over? Was he kidding?

I ran all the way home, but this time I was a harbinger of good news. Words tripped over each other as I explained the whole day's doings. I ate fast because I wanted to start work on next week's "farewell" idea. Cowan was leaving of his own accord, so my being jubilant wasn't at his expense. The next two shows that day were as good as the first and I was talking those clouds again.

But where were Fan and Mike? Weren't they happy with my success? I was a hit where other comics had failed. I was puzzled.

The next day I understood their absence. Louella had caught me again and beat my brains out in her column. I forgot to tell you that all of the other papers, including *Variety*, gave me great notices. I couldn't figure what she wanted of me. Why was she following me around? Lou Edelman had the cheering note, though. He said, "Look, kid, you're not only a hit with the people; the manager from the Ocean Park Theatre was in last night and he wants to play you, too." So, with a mental-nose-thumb to Louella, I was happy again.

On Friday of that week, when I had figured that I'd replace Cowan after he left, Edelman came to me again and told me he was holding me over for a third week. Then he explained that he wanted me to put on a show welcoming the new MC, George Stoll. My chin dropped a foot. What could I say? So I put on the farewell show and the one greeting Stoll. And wouldn't you know that sweet Louella rapped me in her column on every show? I was beginning to get a cauliflower heart.

George Stoll got his hello show and I said goodbye. True to his word, the manager of the Ocean Park Theatre booked me and I did well for him. Fan and Marco came down to the beach to see me with a beautiful one-year contract. What the hell was I crying about? I overcame Louella, didn't I? It was just that so many things had gone awry. I was all mixed up.

My new contract was for fifty-two weeks at Loew's State, with a hundred bucks raise. But before opening, I signed with First National as comic with Georgie Stone and Andy Devine in the last silent film, *Ritzy Rosie.* It starred Alice White and Jack Mulhall. One day Charles Chaplin visited our set and I saw an opportunity. The two-reel comedies had gotten so bad Chaplin had been asked to take over their production at one studio; why couldn't I break into this deal? I broached the subject and he asked me for some comedy ideas. I came up with a funny opening and some gags. Softly the master spoke: "I beg your pardon, Mr. Rubin. May I ask your opinion of a drama I have written?" As I stood open-mouthed he outlined an entire straight-line dramatic story. Before I could comment, he observed: "That, sir, is an outline of the *funniest* picture I ever made. It was called, *The Kid.* If you want to make a good comedy, forget the gags until a straight dramatic story is worked out first." It was an invaluable lesson from a great genius; I have never forgotten it.

After the picture (which gave Andy Devine his 'Gravel-Throat' nickname) I opened at Loew's State, replacing banjo wizard Eddie Peabody.

They had fixed up a suite of rooms for Peabody on the first floor. One was for dressing; one with a couch in it; and the third, kind of a living room. Very elegant! I used all of those rooms, too, but mostly for pinochle, Klabiash and my kibitzing friends and musicians.

On opening day in walked Ruby Keeler. I knew her when she was a bit of a kid and later when she danced in the line (stepping out for specialties) with Flo McFadden (Haley's wife), Mary Crawford and Barbara Stanwyck (Ruby Stevens). After that I saw Ruby Keeler a big success with Texas Guinan. Ruby, her mother and I had a nice reunion. Then she told me she wasn't feeling well and could I stall after her second dance to give her a chance to catch her breath. I did and we had fun doing it. The audience thought it was part of the act.

When the first show was over, a big box of American Beauty roses was delivered to her dressing room. She came to thank me and I told her to save her thanks—I hadn't sent the flowers. She showed me the card; the signature was "Guess who?" We were both mystified. She sent the flowers to a nearby hospital.

After the second, third and fourth shows came a kimono, linked furs and something else. Ruby was really puzzled and so was Mama. While I was taking off my makeup, the doorman announced that Al Jolson was downstairs to see me. I threw on a robe and came down. With Al was one Lew Schreiber.

We greeted each other and he told me he liked some story I was telling. I thanked him and asked what performance he had seen, and he replied, "All four today."

I said, "Now wait a minute, Al. I couldn't possibly entertain you that much." He laughed and said, "I barely knew you were on the stage. I came to see Ruby Keeler.

"Oh," I said, "then you're 'Guess who'."

"Who else?" he answered, and I ran for Ruby's dressing room.

She thought it was a gag. When I convinced her, she got nervous as a cat, picked up all the gifts and came down to see Jolie standing there with Schreiber. She handed Al the gifts and thanked him very much, but said she couldn't accept them. Jolie told her that they were her gifts and she could give them away if she wanted to, but to please accept them as a token of friendship and admiration. Ruby's Ma took the gifts (Jolie put them in her arms) and said goodnight. That looked preety good to Al and he asked Ruby to have supper with him. She declined, saying she had another engagement. Al tried to get her to break the date, but she would not.

Then Al said, "Your friend won't mind, come on."

A voice from behind said, "But I would mind." We all looked towards the guy. Ruby thanked Jolie again and left with Jackie Fields. Al wasn't angry, but he couldn't fathom why she'd go out with a boxer instead of him, even though the guy was welter weight champion of the world.

Later in the week, Ruby did go out with Al and they became very good friends. You know the rest. As for Louella, she eventually apologized, she had me mixed up with a fiddle player who's name sounded like mine and hadn't been nice to his wife.

One night at dinner, a few years later, with Ruby and Al, Jolie's brother, Harry, and his wife were there. George and Ann Levee were coming out later to play bridge. While we were eating chicken, Harry told us of a place in Puente that he could buy. A going cafe with the furnishings, silverware, the works. He figured that he could make a couple of thousand a week with it; and the purchase price was small.

Al liked the idea and said that he would gladly finance the deal. But he thought it was best to be cautious before going ahead. "Why," asked Al, "does the man want to give away such a good investment for so little?"

"He's sick of the place," Harry explained, shrugging his shoulders. "And besides, money doesn't mean anything to him."

"Harry," Al said, "I think you're too gullible."

"Gullible!" Harry yelled. "How much did I eat? Just one lousy piece of chicken!"

During one of many weeks at the Palace with Jack Haley, I got a phone call as follows: "Ello, Mister Rubin, dat's Rabbi Solomon calling. You people from the theayter do wonderful work, with so many benefits. My heart goes out to you for this. Now I wouldn't imposing on you. I have a small temple and we're selling tickets. Would you be so kindly to take twenty tickets, maybe fifteen? It's only ten dollars a ticket and you will help a worthy cause without rushing out to a benefit and maybe catch cold." I told him I'd take five. So help me, it wasn't five minutes before a man was at the stagedoor for the money. Naturally, I didn't tell Jack. Who speaks of charity? or having been taken. A half hour later, Haley got the same kind of call, word for word from a priest with a beautiful Irish brogue. He went for fifty bucks too. He didn't tell me either, till later.

No sooner had the collector gone when Ruth Etting got a call, but Colonel Gimp answered the phone. From the Colonel's yelling (natural voice) we could hear he was getting the familiar treatment. He said, "I don't care if you are an epistical minister, the little lady works too hard for her dough to toss it off." He hollered a little while longer, fell silent a moment and said, "Them is pretty dirty words to call a guy, for an epistical minister." Then he loosened a gang of words that even *I* didn't use as a kid. Then he switched to a very soft tone and invited the caller to come to the stage entrance and he'd give him some money. He had Morris the elevator man go out and bring him two rolls of quarters which he rapped his fists around, but the episcopal minister must have gone into a monastery, cause he never showed.

============

In Vancouver when I was playing the Orpheum circuit there was a team of Negro boys on the bill, named Harris and Holly. Although they were Negroes, they wore blackface makeup on the stage. They had a very funny act which opened with them pushing a piano out on the stage.

The night before we opened, Harris was strickened with appendicitis and ended up in the hospital instead of on stage. Their act was second on the bill and mine next to closing, so I volunteered to help Holly out. I knew their routines and I figured I would have plenty of time to remove the burnt cork and put on straight makeup before I had to do my *own* act.

So we opened with Harris under the ether in a hospital and me in his spot. No announcement was made of the substitution and only the people in the show knew about it.

The next morning I rushed out to buy a newspaper to see what the reviewer had to say about the Harris-Holly act.

The criticism was quite favorable. It said that Harris and Holly on the number two spot in the show had a fast and funny routine with a good dancing finish. "However," the reviewer went on to say, "when it comes to the dialect, it is apparent that the short, stout fellow never saw the Mason-Dixon Line. He should take a few lessons from the little thin one, who is undoubtedly from the Deep South."

I was the little thin one.

Milton Berle didn't originate borrowing jokes, any more than the Russians organized the first "Red Cross." My first recollection of this type of knavery was when Al Herman borrowed from Frank Tinney, and Mel Klee took from Al Herman.

Marty May not only copied Jack Benny's style, but carried a violin he couldn't play and tinted his hair grey like Jack's natural hair. (Benny was grey in his twenties.)

There were many who tried to fill Al Jolson's shoes, but all rattled around in them.

Nine out of ten right now are living off Ritchie Craig and Fred Allen.

The one I enjoyed most, I was a witness to. There was this here guy, who would steal your best joke and wire you to take it out of your act or he would file a formal complaint with the Vaudeville Managers Protective Association. Some poor slobs did, but not Harry Breen.

Breen wrote his own material and that certain joke the guy asked him to take out was his own brain child. Harry sleepered it to Boston (where I was on the bill with the joke thief), confronted the guy and asked, "You make a living talking, don't you?" The guy answered, "Yeh, what of it?" Harry instructed him to "try it with a lisp," then belted him in the mouth. They booked a sister act in his place that night.

You don't see much of that today, other than Shelley Berman doing George Jessel's telephone act, Jerry Van Dyke doing Gene Sheldon's banjo act; these two men comedy teams aping Abbott and Costello and too many gals trying to do Gracie.

We have only one of each doing Lloyd Hamilton, Charlie Chaplin and Harry Langdon.

There's one other guy doing a hell of a job on Lou Holtz, George Jessel, Willie Howard, Harry Hershfield, Abe Reynolds and the writer. His saving grace is, he's a very nice person.

============

In Kansas City the Marx Brothers were playing the Orpheum Theatre. Ben Bernie was on the same bill. I was in town appearing at the Main Street Theatre. We often got together between shows or after the final show.

One evening Zeppo and I had dinner together. He ordered raw oysters and followed with a couple of milk shakes. Then we went to a billiard parlor for a game.

Zeppo, not surprisingly, became ill and I helped him to the theatre and into his dressing room. He got worse and couldn't go on. Having plenty of time before my act at the Main Street, the boys gave me his lines and I agreed to substitute for him. Here is what happened:

RUBIN: (entering)   My name is Sammy Brown and I just got into town!

Before I could say another line, the stage manager walked on, motioning for me to get off. He figured he knew the part better than I did.

STAGE
MANAGER: My name is Sammy Brown and I just got into town!

Bernie had since come into the theatre and was told about Zep's illness. Since he played on the same bill he knew the part forward and backward, so he rushed onto the stage to lend a hand and his voice.

BERNIE: My name is Sammy Brown and I just got into town!

The audience was perplexed but Groucho was hysterical. Then, who should appear but Zeppo, feeling better, forcing himself to carry on. His voice was weak, but brave.

ZEPPO: My name is Sammy Brown and I just got into town!

VOICE FROM
AUDIENCE: Make up your mind. Who the hell *is* Sammy Brown?

PANOOCHI

Eddie Cantor and I left for New York to play the Palace. Our families saw us off. There was a pretty red-haired gal who got on ahead of us and Ida gave Eddie "permission." We went to our room, unpacked, played a few games of casino and went to dinner. There sat the red-haired lady. She knew us both and introduced herself. She was very charming and laughed at our bum jokes, including remarks I was making in Yiddish. (Good thing she didn't understand.) That evening we passed Red in the club car, invited her to dinner and again we had laughs.

Back in our room, Cantor went through his bedtime ritual. He had salve for everything; new kinds of dentifrices, pills, liniments. All I could think of was, "Where does he find room to carry his money?"

Finally the lights were out. My mind was full of jokes, ideas and toppers for our scenes. I was dying to tell them to Eddie but feared to disturb his sleep. More gags came up, and a wonderful bit to do with two Negro boys. Can't wake Eddie. Another ten minutes; now I feel like a cigarette. Nah, might wake the dear boy. Then he started snapping his fingers. Running a song over in his mind? My toes went with the rhythm. He went into what I thought was the second chorus, then the third. What the hell is he doing, a medley? I lighted a cigarette and he jumped up. "In the middle of the night you've got to smoke? Dope fiend, you woke me up!" "You were up," I said, "weren't you just rehearsing a song?"

He became hysterical and explained the finger snapping. Ida snored slightly and Cantor used to snap his fingers to keep her awake until he fell asleep. It was a habit. Okay, I had my chance to tell him the new stuff I'd thought of. He liked it. We played three more games of casino and went to sleep, without the snapping.

The lady we called Red took some more ribbing (especially my Yiddish remarks) and when we got to Chicago said goodbye to us in the language in which I'd been kidding her. Eddie died laughing, while I turned a turkey red.

We arrived in New York on Sunday. Where did actors go on Sunday? You are right if you thought I was going to say, "To play a benefit." However, we arrived too late and went straight to the Palace, with Block and Sully, the Jack Bennys, the Jack Pearls, the Ed Sullivans, Blossom Seeley and Benny Fields.

At intermission, Fields explained that Blossom and he were rehearsing "Girl Crazy" to do on the road. Gregory Ratoff had promoted his wife, Leontovitch, Ben Bernie and Phil Baker for the money to reproduce it. Also, Gregory was going to play the Willie Howard role, but didn't like himself in the part. Would I consider going in the show if Ratoff stepped out? I said no, since Cantor and I were set with our unit and our opening day had been announced. We went in to see the last half of the bill.

On the way to Cantor's apartment atop the Pierre Hotel, Benny and Blossom pitched to me. I was not interested. If you know either one of us Bennys, we are not whispering Jack Smiths. Our pitched voices attracted the others and both of us gave our stories. No one agreed with Fields.

After we supped with Cantor, Fields started again, but was interrupted by Eve Sully's suggestion for a game of Panoochi. Let me explain Panoochi, so you'll get some fun out of the rest of the yarn. Zeppo Marx and I ad libbed this game years before. It was designed only to drive a good card player crazy. Not one word of what was said meant anything, neither did the amount of cards dealt, or held.

Here is an example of dialogue used while one is shuffling the deck: "Do you want to play the back up Jack, or the circulating Queen?" Answer: "Double trevels are good enough for me, or deuces bland." A few cards are dealt and a few turned face up on the table. More of the above prattle until someone asks, "What are you playing?" Then you say, "You can't learn Panoochi by watching. If you keep score for us, you learn fast." The person usually keeps the score, and we drive him crazy with the double talk.

Jack Benny jumped at the chance to play. We tried to get him not to, because Jack is an easy audience and laughs at anything. We feared that some screwy remark from anyone (especially Eve Sully) would break him up and he'd tip the gag off to the Ed Sullivans and the Pearls, who were the only ones not in on it. Jack insisted, so we cut for partners. I got Jack and Eve got Cantor.

Pearl now wanted to know what we were going to play. We gave him the usual routine about score keeping and with paper and pencil he was ready. The first thing that amazed him (after the screwy preliminary questions) was that we cut, high card dealt. Someone with a deuce dealt. Eve commented, "Ganer on nines, blues everlasting seven." Jack Benny bit his lip. Cantor answered, "Look, Eve—get your points but don't Krivet my nines. Bury me a card and call on elevens, thirteen." Pearl gave him thirteen points. Jack Benny was about to let go, and I said, "Up and down the ladder, turn a card bilf to your Krivet, sixty-two." Pearl's eyebrows raised as he wrote that big number down for me. Jack Benny put his handkerchief to his mouth, his eyes tearing. I bawled him out for a lousy play he made yesterday costing me money (I was on a train yesterday). It sobered him.

But Mary knows now that if he holds on much longer he'll give way. So she yells, "Jack!" He gets up and runs into the bathroom. By now Eddie Sullivan is biting a pencil, Sylvia is biting her finger, Fields and Seeley are over in a corner, hysterical. Jesse replaces Jack, picks up his cards and says, "I've got Menden, give me nine." Pearl gives him nine points. Cantor says, "Wait a minute, Jack, he means nine minus!" Pearl just looks from one to another and scratches off Jesse's nine. Eve puts in quickly, "Rubin is sixty-two? Look, Jack, it's eight, six and two!" By this time Jack Benny has composed himself and comes out of the bathroom. At that moment, Cantor and I are hollering at Pearl. Jack Benny can't stand it and goes back. Pearl sees him and turns to me and says, "I think you're the dirtiest louse I ever met! You yell at your best friend over a lousy few bucks, peeeoo!" Before I can square myself, Eve takes Pearl over into a corner. Now we all know that she is framing me, but how, we don't know. Pretty soon he walks over to me, lays a five dollar bill on the table and challenges me to a game of Panoochi. All I can do is accept and wait. Everyone gathers around the table, including Jack Benny, Mary, Pearl's wife, Winnie, who is amazed at his recklessness with five bucks.

I deal and ask him a lot of double talk questions. He looks at Eve, she nods her assent and I start with some foolish words. Pearl yells, "Panoochi" and grabs the money. As he starts to get up happily, I say, "Dribble" and he looks to Eve. She ad libs, "If he dribbles you owe him triple, fifteen dollars." Well, that broke up the joint. Ed Sullivan wrote a column on it the next day.

Seeley and Fields started again with the "Girl Crazy" routine and we argued a bit. Cantor took me in the other room and showed me where a hit show would mean more to me than a few weeks at the Palace. I had been in the Palace many times, so what? More vaudeville. But once a hit in a show and you go into another show. Okay, I took the job.

The timing was perfect as George Jessel had just returned from toastmastering a dinner for the President in Washington and they went into the Palace for a long run. During the run, Eddie put Gracie on the air with him—and that was the beginning of Burns and Allen as real big timers.

============

Some of the greatest yarns I know concern the comics Jack Benny and George Burns.

People ask me if the Jack Benny-George Burns stories are true. Oh, ho, yes they are.

Here's one I'm part of. Jack had wired us that he was coming into Chicago from Milwaukee. George and I were to meet him at two in the morning. I had to get up early. I had a golf date with Harry Langdon so George said he'd meet him. Well, he didn't. Jack was really steamed when he wasn't met. He went to Burns' hotel and banged on the door. George answered him sleepily "come in."

Jack really blew his cool and started calling him names before the door was *half* opened. When he entered the room, there was George standing up in his bed, nude with Jack's wire in his hand. I don't have to tell you how Jack laughs and rolls on the floor.

Wait, I haven't told you the topper. A few months later, Burns wired Jack *he* was coming in from Philadelphia to occupy a twin bed with Jack at the Edison Hotel in New York. Jack timed it beautifully. He was standing up in bed *nude*, with a rose in his teeth. He answered the knock on the door with a coy "come in." It wasn't George, it was the chambermaid.

There are enough guys still around who can verify this episode, so don't call me a liar.

ZEPPO AND HIS BOOZE

Billy Rose and I were living together at the time. We had just come from seeing the opening of "Garrick Gaieties" and while we were eating, Zeppo Marx, Georgie Hale, Broadway dancer-producer, Billy Rose and Harry Kabakoff, a good featherweight boxer from St. Louis, came in. They sat down with us and in a few minutes Zeppo was painting a rosy picture of a party that was just about beginning in a flat occupied by several chorus girls in Brooklyn.

These girls, Zeppo said, have parties that are the talk of the show world, and since they knew Georgie Hale so well we were all invited. None of us was married at the time so we talked ourselves into it. Rose held out for a while; but he finally came along. We started off in Zeppo's big car.

It was a hot summer night and instead of being cooled by the ride, we got hotter. We didn't know until we were halfway to Brooklyn that Zeppo had the heater turned on full force.

Zeppo promised he was through clowning. We turned down a street that led to the Brooklyn Bridge. Instead of going on the bridge, he cut off and went down to the waterfront under the first span.

"The reason I came down here," Zep said, "is to make a stop at a warehouse where we can pick up a couple bottles of pre-war scotch. We oughta take the girls something. We shouldn't walk in empty-handed."

He pulled up in front of an old warehouse. It was a narrow street lighted by one dim greenish street lamp.

"Come on in," Zep insisted. "I want you to see the store of pre-war whiskey they have. It's amazing."

It was such an eerie street that we didn't need much convincing to leave the car and go inside. Zep maneuvered us into a small office with a sour smell. There were no lights, but the street lamp from outside sent the green rays through barred windows into the room.

"I'm sorry," remarked Rose in gentlemanly tones, "that I let you get me into this."

"Zep, get me out of here, and quick." I said.

But the door was suddenly blocked by a monstrous figure. He was about five feet two inches tall, but about the same width around. He had his head shaven and he wore an undershirt revealing arms, shoulders and muscles that made me think of a truckhorse. He took a step into the room. Hale and Kabakoff slipped out.

There was no escape for us. The little giant held out his big arms to prevent our leaving.

"Now, Elly," Zeppo said nervously, "don't get excited, these are my friends."

Elly threw his arms up and bellowed like a bull with a Teutonic accent: "No! No! Dey are poleezmens. Dey vant to take Elly. Dey vant to ruin his beeziness-ss!"

Scared half to death, I started talking fast, pleading with Elly to believe we were not policemen and that I had been there before and had met him.

Elly glared and scowled. He advanced and laid his huge fist against my chest.

"You are poleezmens, ya! Und soo—I will keel you. I keel all poleezmens what come here. Ya, I got nunteen upschtairs!"

"You're mistaken, Elly, my friend," I said, affecting a brave air, "I am not a policeman. I'm an actor." I yelled for Zeppo to call him off. But there was no Zeppo. Rose and I were alone in the room with Elly—and he thought we were cops.

Suddenly the place was filled with eerie noises. There was the sound of chains rattling, feet pounding on the ceiling, screams for help. All I could think of was those 19 policemen, still alive upstairs and trying to get out. I yelled again for Zeppo.

Elly now seized my neck with one of his powerful hands. He reached for Rose with the other. "I am going to keel you. I won't let you suffer."

I pleaded again that I was a comedian and dancer, and that the little guy with me was a song-writer.

"I give you von chance. You vill show me."

So while Billy sang, I danced. I kept interrupting the song to scream "Zeppo!" Then the hellish noises broke loose again and I looked at Elly and he was a horrible sight. He was frothing at the mouth and staggering toward me. He seized me, fell upon me and we went down. I don't know where I got the strength, but I crawled out from under him, grabbed Billy by the hand and we ran out of the door and into the street. There, by the light of the greenish lamp, we saw Zeppo, Harry and Georgie.

"Thank God, you're alive," Zeppo said hoarsely, "we have no time to lose. The man is mad." We scrambled into the car and slammed the doors. It was just in time. Elly was coming at us with the biggest crowbar I had ever seen.

Now Zep couldn't get the car started. I was petrified. Elly reached the car and raised his weapon. He was about to strike a crushing blow when he frothed at the mouth, wavered and fell to the sidewalk. Zep got the car going and we roared down the street.

I was mad now. I started cursing Zeppo. I said I would fight him, Georgie and the boxer all at once for bringing us to such a place.

Zeppo replied calmly. "Well, if you're that tough, why didn't you fight Elly?"

"I was just about to hit him when he had that fit," I said.

"You know, it's odd," Zeppo went on quietly, "but everybody I bring down here says the same thing."

I noticed Kabakoff was holding a handerchief to his mouth. Georgie had his head buried in his arms, and he was laughing, too.

It slowly dawned on me. The whole thing was a rib. I swallowed and gulped: "I suppose you fellows think I didn't know it was a gag all along. I knew it from the beginning."

This brought Billy Rose's first remark during the entire episode: "Why didn't you tell me, Benny?"

Billy didn't talk to any of us for a long time. I later learned that the warehouse was a stable and the tramping of feet were the horses being disturbed by Kabakoff. Georgie and Zep made the other noises and beat chains on the floor. Elly was the night watchman who was always paid $10.00 by Zep to do his act. His foaming at the mouth was effected by a powder Zep purchased at a drugstore.

Billy produced many shows after that, hired a lot of comics and many dance producers. But the Marx's, Georgie Hale and I never were in any of them. Not until years later was I to work for him in the Diamond Horseshoe, though he neither saw nor hired me.

============

This one concerns two acrobats who nearly killed themselves at every performance.

First, what bugged them was, they either opened or closed the show; which meant they were performing while people were being seated, or playing to the backs of the people who were leaving.

After one particular matinee, they were in their dressing room under the stage, trying to dry off, while catching their breath.

The third act—Robert Warwick—in a dramatic sketch was getting thunderous applause.

One of them said, "What does that guy up there do to get that?"

The other one said, "I don't know, he don't do no tricks, or hoof or nothing, else we could hear it down here. Whew!"

The other one said, "When we get through tonight leave us stay up there and see what the bum does."

After they did their act that night, they took a position where they could see and hear.

For twenty minutes they listened to Warwick's deep, resonant voice painting pictures with words. Then, at the finish of a bombastic speech, with great dramatic power, boom! the house rocked with applause.

One acrobat said, "Ya hear that! That's the kind of crap we'll do next year."

============

It was a legit actor that made life miserable for vaudevillians.

David Warfield was a close friend of Marcus Loew and even closer with a buck. He had purchased a lot of "Loew's Incorporated" stock and went with Mr. Loew to inspect a new theatre out of town.

They got there in time to see as many people outside of the theatre as there were in it. He was the man who gave Mr. Loew the idea for the supper show. The acts did three a day instead of two, for the same dough. Then came the fancy name of "presentation" houses. They put a movie in between the acts doing four shows a day. All I'll tell you about it is the one guy that beat the rap—Joe Jackson.

Joe was the funniest pantomimist of his time. His act consisted of a tramp trying to steal a bicycle. Then he performed great tricks on it, even though it fell apart as he rode it.

Joe had a son who could do the act as well as he did and they'd either alternate shows or one would do the matinee and the other the evening performance.

At the Roxy one afternoon, Joe Senior stood in the back of the house talking to the manager. The manager looked at his watch and said, "Joe, you've only got fifteen minutes till you go on." Joe shrugged it off with, "I can make it in five." Three minutes later the manager took Joe into the lobby and pushed him toward the street saying, "Come on, Joe, don't do this to me." Joe said, "I'll tell you what I'll do. I'll bet you five bucks I leave here five minutes before I go on and I'll make it." The manager urged, "Joe, I don't want your money, but I know it takes you longer than that to put on your makeup." Joe answered, "Not if I take a cab." With that, he jumped into a taxi and sped off.

The manager ran around the block, found the stage manager and hurriedly told him to revise the show, Jackson wouldn't make it.

From behind him came a voice, saying, "Why not?" It was Joe Jackson in full makeup and the manager almost fainted.

But it was not Joe Senior, it was Joe Junior. Senior was on his way to a ball game.

=============

This is about Germany's strongman act. A real, honest to

goodness superman. He was the most powerful fellow I ever met. His act consisted of bending iron bars over the back of his neck by grasping the ends and pulling forward; until the bar was shaped like a horseshoe.

One night, he was complaining because he had an audience which was sitting on its hands. He had just bent a half inch bar to no applause, and as he was walking upstage to get another bar, those of us in the wings could hear him mumbling: "Gott damn Americans . . . dey only know to laugh at farshtoonkeh jokes! Der iss no culltduar."

He walked down to the footlights, scornfully bounced his second bar on the stage, and growled to the audience: "Deese iss vun injhes dick un zolid irrron." He seized the bar, and literally wrapped it around his neck. Still there was only a smattering of applause.

"Gott damn American svine," he muttered. "No applause; must be frrom der last var der feeling is shtill hevvy." Then he picked up a piece of iron which resembled a crowbar, and strode majestically downstage. This time he announced: "Ladies oond beeple. Diss bar isss two injhes dick!"

He took a handerchief from the top of his tights, laid it across the back of his neck, put the bar in place, and pulled, with groans and grunts, until the two "injhes" of bar bent into a "v" shape. The audience let out an avalanche of cheers. The strongman dropped the bar, touched the tips of his fingers together, and placed them under his chin. Then, coyly it seemed, he skipped offstage. He did not return for a bow, although he got great applause.

The manager of the theatre ran up the side aisle and backstage into the strongman's dressing room. There was the German, still daintily poised, holding his jaw.

The manager cried, "Why the hell are you sitting there like a chorus girl? Aren't you cute, with your pretty hands under your chin? You get out there, and take a bow!"

The Heinie answered: "I could not dake des bow effen if I wished . . . oond mine hands iss like diss . . . because I brroke mine gott damn neck!"

============

Dezzo Retter was a comedian who vas also mit a dialect but I zink so an Amerrrican zitissner. Anyway he did a hilarious act. He wore a gym costume and pads formed phoney muscles under the long sleeves of his tights. He would come out on the stage and start to wrestle with himself.

A fellow named Harry Cooper who was well known for his "Empire City Quartette," but won even more renown for his great charity work, asked a group of us vaudevillians to take part in his pet show—a Thanksgiving Day affair on Blackwell Island for the New York "Laughing Academy" as Bugs Baer used to call it.

We were assigned a car to ourselves on the train and were cutting up touches about show business and people who make it. Dezzo tried to get into the conversation with stories about vaudeville back in Berlin. We didn't give him a chance, interrupting with double talk and shooting it to him in his dialect. Finally he got tired of it all and said he would go up ahead into the smoker.

He left and went into the next car. But it wasn't the smoker. He sat down with about 20 patients who were mentally deranged and who were accompanied by a couple of guards.

When the train arrived at the Island, a guard started to count heads. He counted to five and came to Dezzo. "Who are you?" he asked.

Dezzo recited: "I am Dezzo Rrretter, der man vhat rezzels mit himseluff."

The guard went on counting six, seven, eight, nine, etc.

We had gotten back stage in the auditorium and had started to hang up our clothes and arrange our props before Cooper missed Retter. Then the hunt began. Finally he was located in a padded cell doing his act and screaming at the guards trying to explain it. The more he yelled and more furiously he wrestled, the more hopeless his case became until he had completely convinced the keepers that he was nuts.

Cooper straightened everything out and Dezzo was released but he positively refused to do the show for fear other guards might think he was daffy and lock him up again.

============

Here's another one that concerns Benny and Burns. I am

kind of in it too.

It was 1931 in Chicago. Jack was starring in Earl Carroll's Vanities. I was starring in "Girl Crazy." He was asked to do a fifteen minute spot on radio. The medium was strange to him, so he asked me to go along for moral support. We couldn't possibly get a cab so we walked thru a blizzard to get to the radio station. Jack had prepared eleven minutes for himself and three minutes for Harry Stockwell to do a song. The other minute I guess was for station identification. By the way, Dean and Guy Stockwell are Harry's sons.

Well, Stockwell didn't get there because he wouldn't risk his voice walking in a blizzard. During a break, I told Jack I'd fill the three minutes for him. He was to announce an imitation of me and then I'd step in and do the funniest joke I knew.

We did exactly that, and the next day the newspapers reviewed Jack's appearance like this: "Jack Benny was very refreshing and funny on his initial radio stint, until he did an imitation of Benny Rubin, that was simply awful.

Jack called George Burns that night and explained the whole bit. George listened attentively and said, "You shouldn't leave home without your writers," and hung up.

I guess you've heard it a hundred times, George used to take a delight in hanging up on Jack. It wasn't out of meanness, he knew the abruptness of *anything* made Jack laugh. Here, I'll give you an idea of how it worked. Another time Jack and I were here in Hollywood, he said he wanted to call George in New York and have some laughs, but was afraid he'd hang up on him again. I bet Jack twenty bucks that Burns *wouldn't* hang up.

So Jack called George and told him a joke. George laughed and Jack said you didn't hang up on me, you know you just cost we twenty bucks! I bet Benny Rubin you would hang up on me.

Burns said, "I know, I've got half of his bet."

============

No matter who you were, or how long you'd been around, you just couldn't have played on the bill with everybody. There were some greats I'd have given my left ear to know personally. One was Chief Capaulican.

I had seen this big handsome Indian from front, and heard that magnificent basso profundo voice rock the theatre.

When I read in *Variety* that I was going to be on the bill with him and his band at the Palace, I was thrilled.

Came nine o'clock Monday at orchestra rehearsal, I was there. Usually I didn't show till after ten because my rehearsal was a soft touch. Bring me on with "Reuben Reuben I Been Thinkin," tacit for fourteen minutes and "I'll See You In My Dreams," stop-time for a dancing finish.

I listened to the dog act rehearse, "Where, O Where Has My Little Dog Gone," watched the trapeze act put up their rigging and heard a mild beef between the Siamese twins. Oh, oh, here they come.

Indians in street dress, lugging their instruments thru the stage door and last but not least my hero. The stalwart chief moved stealthily among his braves and talked. Pretty soon, he lit a big cigar and strode over to where I was standing.

"Chief," I said, "I have been a great admirer of yours." He puffed his cigar and stared at me. "Were all of you born on reservations?" He looked away and spoke to an Indian who was fingering the valves on his trumpet. "Oiving, dis tendafeet vants to know from vich reservation do ve coming?" Oiving replied, "So give him a Pictserr and let be like dat." I bit my lips. The big chief looked down at me. "Mine boy eff anybody vill esk you, tell dem ve are Shmokawks. Awribberderchie."

============

Look out now, I'm going to get sexy with you. If you're under seven take this into the nursery. If over fifty, take some LSD.

We had what we called "girl acts." There were boy performers too, but the feature was showing off the girl's charms.

Then there were troupes of various kinds that also sold girls.

I don't care what kind of a company it was, there was always a louse to oversee that there was no hanky panky. Either the owner of the act or some stool pigeon kept a watchful eye in the hotels.

So what did we do? We beat the rap on trains.

Picture a sleeping car. The men's is up there and the ladies' is down there at the other end. The porter sat at the men's end, where he could see the entire car. This guy was usually a benevolent church going man; however he was also devoted to money. So for a few bucks he became a policeman for the owner.

Just suppose it was me who had a tryst with Trixie Hicks. I'd go to the men's room and call to the porter to help me with something. The second he left his post, Trixie came into my pad. When the switchback had to be made, "I'd pass the porter in such a way he saw the quarter in my hand. I gave a little holler, he follered. Trixie made her move. Sounds easy, huh? Don't ever try it when you're in uppers. Trixie still had the scar on her leg when she arrived at Loews Heaven.

I'm sure that the conductor on the big train in the sky gave her a lower on cloud nine.

============

Again, two hoofers. We'll call them Guppy and Fogg. Let's eavesdrop on them.

GUPPY:	Fred, we gotta do somethin to get us out of that deuce spot so we'll get some billing. That way maybe we can nail a Broadway show.
FOGG:	We don't do nuthin that'll get us a better spot. But I know what we can do.
GUPPY:	Wha?
FOGG:	Leave us get pally with a headliner. If they happen to like ya, they'll throw in a plug someplace.
GUPPY:	I know what ya mean. Mix with men ya get money, mix with lice ya get lousy.
FOGG:	I couldna said it no better.

The following day they were in a railroad station and who did they see waiting for the same train? Wilton Lackeye.

GUPPY:	Hey, there's Wilton Lackee the legit star; let's give him a rumble.
FOGG:	Go ahead, you always do the talk-in for the act.
GUPPY:	Hello, Mr. Lackee, we seen ya a hunnert times and you're the nuts.
MR. LACKEYE:	Oh . . . yes . . . thank you.
FOGG:	We're in your racket too, only we're hoofers, no legit.
MR. LACKEYE:	Gentlemen, forgive me if I am not too communicative. I am quite sad, I just lost my father.
GUPPY:	Hey! That's a coincidence, we just lost our trunk.

============

George Burns makes you laugh with these kind of lies, but it is still true of vaudevillian's thinking:

JERRY:	Did ya hear about Jackie Dean replacing Sinatra in Vegas when he got sick, and was a smash hit?
TERRY:	I diddn hear.
JERRY:	You must of heard when he jumped in for Liberace when he lost his candelabra and they held him over for five weeks.
TERRY:	I diddn hear.
JERRY:	How about when he was booked on his own and bombed so bad they cancelled him after the first show.
TERRY:	This I heard.

95

FOREIGN TRADE

Ann Codee, who became famous with Frank Orth in vaude-ville as "Orth and Codee," came to America on her first trip with her troupe of girls. They had been a sensation as an acrobatic dancing act in the Folies Bergere in Paris. They opened at the Hippodrome in New York in their customary attire; beautiful, sheer pink silk sleeveless tights. They received a terrific ovation, melting into uproarious laughter. Since the act was not supposed to get laughs, the girls were bewildered. But they carried on their brilliant dancing and amazing tricks. They went off with tumultuous applause but even this was mingled with laughter.

Back stage, the girls were broken-hearted, crying bitterly at the strange reception by an American audience. At this point their manager entered. He calmed the group and after clearing his throat a couple of times, he took the plunge. In France, he told them, delicately, sleeveless tights were popular even though the ladies never heard of an underarm depilatory, but in America it was different. Razors had to be used if costumes were sleeveless or sheer as theirs were.

The ladies became indignant, then furious. But the manager insisted. There followed an hysterical scene and the girls cried, "Let us go home—let us go back to Paris!" But eventually the manager had his way. You conjure up in your mind, five girls shaving thru tears. It was a gas!

They won their audiences and stayed in the United States for a long time. They came to love America, of course, and often laughed at their earlier embarrassment.

But after a while they had to return to France. And the day

they opened again in Paris there was a great ovation. But immediately the reception subsided. They finished their act in abysmal silence. Again came the tears in the dressing room, again came the manager to explain. There followed a busy few minutes as they scurried about for bits of crepe hair to glue on properly in order to placate the disappointed Parisians. Some switch, eh?

OPPORTUNITY KNOCKS ONCE

Seed and Austin had a hell of a finish to their act, which had to do with one bragging about his bravery. The punch line was, when Ben Schaeffer (a stooge) in a huge bear skin would enter and chase him off stage.

They were on seventeenth, on an eighteen act bill at Willi Hammersteins. Ben Schaeffer had the bear skin on and carried the bear head in his hand as the opening act went on. A little more than two hours later when Seed read the cue line for Ben to enter and chase him, there was no Ben and the act died. They went off to nothing. As they broken-heartedly climbed the stairs to their dressing room they encountered Ben running down.

Austin screamed, "Where the hell were you?" Ben honestly answered, "I had to go back to the dressing room, I forgot to put on my jockstrap!"

YOU'LL LEARN NOTHING HERE

Jack Dempsey took two trainloads of Hollywoodites to Reno for his twenty-round fight between Paulino Uzcudun and a big new comer by the name of Max Baer. On our train there were plenty of laughs—and a few heartaches too. The card game losses in some instances were fabulous. I know, because I had ten percent of Zeppo's play. On the way up I won a chunk. On the way back Zeppo wasn't so lucky and we blew it back.

The morning before the fight, one very stuffy producer's wife suggested going slumming. The other gals thought it would be fun envisioning quaint and historical places and a chance to buy some antiques. Instead, they blundered into the red light district. Some of the gals were outside of their cribs sunning themselves and cutting up touches. Everything was serene until the stuffy one adjusted her lorgnettes and gave out with, "Oh my heavens, Prostitutes!" One of the babes called over, "You lookin' for your daughter, lady?" That was all.

Back around the hotel the boys were enjoying themselves. One gassed guy pushed another into a swimming pool. I quickly took my watch off my wrist and handed it to Tom Kennedy. (You've seen him in lots of pictures.) Tom was Dempsey's partner in the fight venture. Someone saw me hand Tom my watch and almost everybody followed suit. Before it was over, Buster Keaton, Eddie Mannix, Nat Deverich, Zeppo, Chico, Jack Warner, Darryl Zanuck, Cantor—well, almost everybody had been dunked. Dempsey walked into the scene, saw Tom laughing his head off, sneaked up behind him and—there was Kennedy in the water with all of our watches in his pocket. We pushed Dempsey in too, natch!

The fight was a gruelling one. Dempsey had a sixteen foot ring erected, instead of a twenty-two, and the fighters couldn't get out of each other's way. I don't remember who won it, but I do remember one crack. Uzcudun complained to Dempsey who was the referee, "He butt me!" Dempsey judiciously advised, "Butt him back." He did and at the end they both looked like dolls.

TOM DUGAN

Oh, how I wish you could have known Tommy Dugan. Maybe, some of you do. He did a great vaudeville act and I guess he was in more than a hundred movies.

This sweet loveable guy was soft spoken and very charitable, BUT he had the most *insane* sense of humor I ever heard.

Here's just *one* of the daffy things he did. There was a ragtime piano player he was nuts about. This guy lived to eat, and was very gruff in his speech. One night in a restaurant in New York, Tommy said, "I'm going to have a steak, smothered in onions, a baked potato, apple pie and coffee."

His friend said, "Order me the same thing, but instead the baked potato, I want two orders french fries, I'm gonna wash my hands."

After he left the table, Tommy called the waitress and said to her. "Miss, I'm a doctor, the man who'll be eating with me is my patient. He mustn't eat meat or fried potatoes, so try and get him to eat milk toast, or crackers and milk. Now! I'll have a sirloin steak, smothered in onions and two orders of french fries. Coffee now and milk for him."

The guy came back to the table and said, "Did you order for me?" Tom nodded his head as the waitress brought Tom coffee and the other fellow milk.

He said, "Wait a minute, how come ya give him coffee and me milk?"

The waitress sweetly said, "That's what the doctor ordered."

He said, "I don't know nuttin from no doctor and I ain't no pussy cat. Gimme some coffee." Tom nodded yes, to the waitress.

She said, "Okay, I'll bring your coffee in a minute. Now, what are we going to have for dinner?"

He said, "We? I don't know about *you*, but I'll tell ya what *I'm* gonna have. The biggest steak what ya got, smothered. . . ."

The waitress asked, "Wouldn't you like some nice milk toast instead?"

"Get oudda here. You like milk toast, eat it yourself, look a you. . . ."

Tom said, "Excuse me I've got to wash my hands." On the way out, Tom said to the manager of the restaurant, "Your waitress is having trouble with my patient, see if you can get him to have some milk toast." Then he disappeared.

The manager came to the table in time to hear the guy say, "Look a lady, bring me the meat and potatoes, will ya?"

The manager told the waitress he'd handle it from now on and she left. The manager said, "Now then how would you like some *nice* milk toast?"

The guy answered, "And how would you like a belt right in the puss?"

The manager said, "Now, now, now, let's not get physical."

The guy (crying), "Oh, mister, don't make me break my hands on ya, will ya? I make a livin playin piano. . . . Hey, what's this here?"

The waitress brought a large steak, the onions and the french fries and set it down where Tom had been seated.

The manager said to the waitress, "I thot . . ." She cut in, "*This* is for the *doctor*," and she took off.

The guy pulled the platter to him and said, "Oh, the doctor, huh? Well *goody* for the *doctor*." And cut into the steak.

At that moment Tom returned; the manager said, "Doctor, you'll have to handle the patient yourself!" He left.

The guy with a mouth full of food said, "Yeh, doctor sit down and watch the patient take him medicine, ho, ho, ho, ho."

Tom sat there with a silly grin on his face. Then the waitress set before him a bowl of milk and some crackers.

She sing-songed, "This is what the doctor ordered." If you knew Tom, he *rarely* laughed out loud, but this time he really let go with a holler and don't you know, he ate the crackers and milk?

=============

The second time I was on the bill with Dugan and Raymond. Tom Dugan, the originator of double talk, and I were walking to the theatre after dinner. A stranger was coming down the street toward us, minding his own business. Tom brushed me aside and accosted the stranger.

"Well, how have you been?" He grabbed the man's hand.

"I'm fine," replied the other, dismayed, "but . . ."

"You certainly do look fine after 15 years."

"I feel fine," said the man, "but aren't you—?"

"Have I got something to tell you!" Tom jumped in before the guy could finish. He grabbed the man firmly by the arm and headed him toward the theatre. I ran on ahead to tell the other actors that some fun was coming their way.

"You know I'm not down at the other place any more." Tom told his victim. "I'm in show business now. See, that's my name up there in lights and I'm making plenty of money!"

"Wait a minute," the man said determinedly. "I am afraid you are making a mis—"

"How's Harry?" Tom interrupted.

"Harry? Harry who?"

"Oh, you know—Harry. Harry—what's his name?"

"Do you mean Harry Clark?"

"Yeah, that's the guy. Is he still married?" Now they were walking up the alley toward the stage entrance.

"Now look," said the man trying to draw back. "Before we go any further—you must have me mixed up with—"

"Say, you haven't told me a thing about yourself!" Tom rattled on. He now had him inside and on the way to his dressing room. The rest of us left our doors ajar.

The fellow was saying, "Are you sure you don't have me confused—"

"Come in and sit down," Tom ordered. Dugan sat in a chair in front of his makeup table and mirror. He seated his guest on a flat top trunk only two feet away so that he would look right into Tom's face in the mirror.

Then Tom made five pink dots on his face with a stick of grease paint. Suddenly he screamed. Then he whispered, hoarsely,

"Crazy business, isn't it?" and laughed insanely.

"Look, mister," the victim whined. "You don't know me and I better get out of here!"

"Not before I tell you one thing," Tom said mysteriously. "You know that I love kids. You cannot have children when you travel, can you? No. But my wife is stubborn and so *she* had the kid anyway."

"What's wrong with that?" the man asked nervously.

Tom had now smoothed grease paint over his face. He put some brown shadow in the hollow of each cheek and turned, putting his face close to the poor stranger's.

"It had three feet, so I killed it!"

The man leaped to his feet. Tom pushed him down by the shoulders. "Don't create a scene. Someone might hear us."

"You're nuts! Let me out of here," the man shouted.

"Not until you take the baby," said Tom menacingly. "I'll give you fifty bucks to carry it out of here. I have it wrapped up in that trunk you are sitting on, and you're in this as much as me."

The poor man leaped off the trunk, pushed Tom out of the way, opened the door and ran smack into Miss Raymond, Tom's partner. She clutched at his arms and screamed, "Where is my baby?"

"He's got it in the trunk!" the man shouted hysterically, pointing toward Tom who was standing in the doorway with an amused smile. The fellow tore himself from Miss Raymond's grasp and fled from the theatre.

============

Harry Ruby, the composer, suggested a baseball game for charity. Ruby could think baseball when you're making routine sex talk. Okay, a ball game it was.

The late Jack Lelivelt, manager of the Los Angeles Angels got Mr. Fleming to give us Wrigley Field for the game. We got to the actors and publicity departments. Bob Cobb, owner of the Brown Derby, gave us a dinner and a private room for our first meeting, when we discussed players, plays and comedy. Marty Fiedler gave us his soft ball field (he originated girl's baseball) to practice on and rehearse our comedy. To the stars who had never played ball, we gave private lessons. We publicized the game over radio and in newspapers. Tickets sold for as high as one thousand dollars for four box seats.

On the day of the game—"Leading Men *vs* Comedians," for Mt. Sinai Hospital—I was at the park at eight in the morning laying out dressing rooms, uniforms, and shoes, rehearsing prop men for trick gags, radio people for the broadcast, checking the P A system, the Goodrich Rubber Company's dirigible for a gag with Buster Keaton.

The actors showed up around noon. I called a meeting about the gags and gave warnings about "throwing out arms" before the game and sliding with spiked shoes. They practically booed me with, "I played college ball, I played high school ball, I tried out once for a pro team." "Okay," I said, "take your best shots." Out they went. One showed up late and surprised me—my boss, partnered with Harry Cohn at Columbia Pictures, Sam Briskin, bedecked in uniform and wearing a mitt. He claimed he was a shortstop. I almost laughed, but the guy amazed me afield.

Here, as I recall, are the lineups:

Comedians	Leading Men
Buster Keaton	George Raft
Jimmy Phalen	Dennis Morgan
Harry Ruby	Walter Abel
Joe E. Brown	Ricardo Cortez
Sam Briskin	Frank Shields (tennis player)
Vince Barnett	John Boles
Wally Vernon	Vic Orsatti
Charlie Winninger	James Cagney
Ernie Orsatti	Jackie Coogan
Max Rosenbloom	Arthur Treacher
Allen Jenkins	Bing Crosby
Andy Devine	Richard Arlen
Ritz Brothers	Dick Powell
Jack Benny	Jackie Cooper
Mitchell and Durant	Billy Bakewell
Al K. Hall	Lucien Hubbard
Lucien Littlefield	
Sid Silvers	

George Jessel   <u>Umpires</u>
Benny Baker

Lon Chaney
James Gleason
Dewey Robinson
Jack La Rue
Boris Karloff

The field was cleared; the P A system announced the umpires, who came on to boos. They all had guns and menaced the audience. Then, James Cagney and John Boles, as people cheered. They played catch while others were introduced, two at a time. Jackie Coogan and Dick Powell and so on.

The comics' first hitter was Buster Keaton, with four or five bats. The first ball he hit disappeared in the bat. The next one exploded and Bus did a pratt fall. The third ball he hit sharply; it soared into the air and a parachute opened on the ball. While it was descending, Bus made a home run.

The Ritz Brothers came up, sitting on each other's shoulders. Each had a bat and all three were called out on strikes. They hopped the umpires, who chased them with guns. There were many gags, but how we handled the leading men was this.

To begin with, you made suckers out of them as soon as you put them in uniform. There is no way to tailor them to make the darlings look good. So we made them heroes with ball and bat! Any ball they socked went through the infield for base hits. And they were allowed to score.

Four guys didn't need any help. Frank Shields had hits each time up, so did Coogan. But Jimmy Cagney and Dennis Morgan were the long-ball sluggers.

One of my pitches hit Georgie Raft on the leg and he refused to take a base, hitting safely anyway. Vince Barnett broke his leg sliding. And Joe E. Brown shot himself in the hand with a blank, burning his fingers. He was to have shot a leading man trying to steal second.

I announced that Gabby Street had caught a ball, thrown from the top of the Washington Monument in Washington, D. C.— but Buster Keaton was going to catch a ball from the dirigible. The field was cleared and Bus stood at second base. The boys in the blimp got their cue from me, and dropped two dozen tennis balls. Gauging the wind, they hit Bus and second base better than a bomb sight. Bus did a flip and came up with a ball in his mouth.

The game resumed. I announced that Billy Bakewell was pinch-hitting for Richard Arlen. The audience looked to the dugout for Bakewell, but the gate in left field opened and a long limousine drove up to home plate.

The footman and chauffeur leaped to the doors as Billy stepped out. He wore tails, top hat, white tie, white gloves, carried a cane. His men took his gloves and cane. They handed him a bat and Billy took his stance at the plate. A ball was lobbed up and he swung from his heels. The ball dribbled to Wally Vernon, who fumbled on purpose. Billy was *driven* to first base. He stole second. He stole third. By now every player had a ball in his hand. They slowly sneaked over to third base and Billy. They dared him to steal home. Billy took off for home plate, with nine guys chasing him. When he got there, everyone tagged him at once. You couldn't see Billy under the pile. At the right time, the boys spread out and Billy walked stoically to the dugout, wearing only a high hat and jockstrap. The umpires started shooting in all directions and the game was over.

Well, a worthy charity was a lot richer.

COHAN AND THE BOOZERS

Mickey and Larry were two of the best hoofers in vaudeville. They were also two of the best bottle men you'd find in any alley. At this particular time they were in an alley where George M. Cohan had just emerged from a stage entrance. The following dialogue ensued:

MICKEY: Hey, George, how about borrowing a fin?

GEORGE: I don't give money to drunks.

MICKEY: Larry, throw a louse on him.

Larry grabbed Mickey's arm and dragged him back to their room in the flea bag hotel.

LARRY: I was never so embarrassed in my life the way you insulted Mr. Cohan.

MICKEY: Well, he didn't give us nothin, did he?

LARRY: Shut up. I'm gonna write him a letter and apologize.

MICKEY: Do what ya want. I don't care. Where'd you hide the bottle?

LARRY: In my shoe, the one what ain't got a hole in it. Gimme the Bible, I'm gonna use it for a dictionary.

He wrote:

Dear Mr. Cohan:

It behooves me verily to impart to thee, I do not condone my partner's verbiage. I pray of thee to have compassion and be merciful for his righteousness sake. May thou dwell in the house of the Lord and show him forgiveness as we forgive our debtors.

                              Most ecclesiastically,

                              Larry Berns

P.S. And that ain't no bull shit!

                ============

An agent you know, was talking about a girl I wish I knew to a casting executive.

AGENT: Charlie, I got a chick sittin in your outer office that's dynamite!
CASTER: Tell me.
AGENT: She goes fifty five, twenty three, thirty two.
CASTER: What has she done?
AGENT: No acting experience.
CASTER: Then what? Does she sing or dance?
AGENT: No.
CASTER: Well, what does she do?
AGENT: I think I can get her to sit up.

IS THAT WHO YOU THINK YOU ARE? WELL YOU AIN'T

The name of the producer in this story shall be nameless, only because he deserves to be. But the name of Joe Laurie, Jr. will be remembered forever, because love goes on forever.

George M. Cohan and Sam Harris had written glowing letters of introduction, telling a Hollywood producer of the great talents of Joe and how he could be of great value to the man, as a writer, actor. They also timed telegrams to the producer to be delivered the morning of Joe's arrival in Hollywood. Joe got off the train, phoned the producer and his secretary, told Joe to come right out to the studio—they were expecting him.

Joe grabbed a cab, checked his bags in a "near-by the studio restaurant" and hurried up to the information desk. He didn't want to keep the big man waiting.

Sure enough, there was a pass for him to enter the studio and go right to the producer's office. On the way he stopped at a vending machine, smoothed his hair, straightened his tie and ran his finger down his—but he needn't have had, he was dressed properly.

Very composed he entered the office and introduced himself to the secretary. She was glad to see him and immediately announced into the interoffice com in perfect diction that Joe Laurie, Jr. had arrived.

With his own ears he heard the reply, "Ask Mr. Laurie to wait a few minutes." It was 9:45 a.m. by the solid gold antique clock on the wall. Joe fingered through some box office magazines, the *Variety*, and a complete volume of books on *How to Beat Your Help Into Subservience*. It was now 12 o'clock.

The secretary repaid his patience with a great big smile as she responded to a buzzer call and disappeared into the great one's sanctorium.

When she returned Joe stood up and he was ready to go in for his interview. But the secretary bade him go have some lunch as the great one was called into conference.

Joe thought that that would be good because he might run into some people he knew who worked there and he could cut up some touches.

Then she told him that outsiders were not allowed in the commissary and that he could find a nice restaurant off the lot. And please take his time as the big one would have lunch after the conference. She added, "Two o'clock, shall we say?"

So Joe joined his baggage in the "near-by the studio" restaurant and did take his time. In fact, he had to because he had to wait for a stool and his waitress also was in the conference with a guy she was stuck on, who sits way down there near the coffee urns. While he was waiting for his food, he called Arthur Unger—who was head of *Variety* office at the time.

When he got the food the hamburger was cold and dry and the cheese on top had frozen to a rubber heel texture. Ee'n though he got indigestion the laugh was on the waitress because Joe had ordered lox on a bagel.

Now it was five minutes of two and Joe had obeyed every request to the letter, to wit—hurry out to the studio, wait a few minutes, go to lunch, take your time, and, "Two o'clock, shall we say?"

At two sharp he entered the office, sat down again, smiled again, she smiled back again and he read the same magazines again. But this time what he read was red.

Then he remembered the sage sayings of the erudite philosophers Harry Ruby and Violinsky. "He what is pulling his hair is blowing the race to the tortoise." And the *Summum Bonum*: "He that thinketh evil must wind up in the water closet."

Cogitating these words calmed Joe down as he hummed to himself. "Oh how I laughed when I think how I cried about you."

If that gold antique clock had chimes it would have rung four o'clock. However, Joe knew it was four o'clock because he heard from the inner office radio words, "They're all in the starting gate for the fifth race."

One minute and twenty-two seconds later, Joe was startled to hear from the inner office language that he hadn't heard since the time the curtain descended on Tallulah's head.

The secretary smiled sweetly at Joe and Joe returned the smile but this time with only half of his teeth. She then pressed the little button on the inter com and announced sweetly that Mr. Joe Laurie, Jr. was still waiting. Then to Joe's amazement, he heard the man say, "Send him in." Joe didn't flinch, he straightened up to his greatest height, which was about five feet three inches and entered the spacious office of the man who could change his whole life, yet couldn't pick a horse in the money. "Sit down," said the man. Joe sat down but he looked very awkward sitting down with one arm extended because his hand was empty of the handshake he had offered. Not only that, but the leather cushion in the seat slowly sank beneath his weight giving off a soft hissing sound. You see, Joe was used to applause.

Joe wasn't eavesdropping, mind you, but there in cold black print on yellow Western Union paper he saw his name bulge out. (You know, like when you see your name in a column.)

"Now," said the big man, "What's your name?"

You know how a drowning man sees his whole life before him just as he's going down for the third time? Well, Joe didn't go through that bit, but what he did do was take inventory of George M. Cohan and Sam Harris calling this man on the phone using his name ten times, his name was emblazoned on the telegrams and the secretary had said, "Mr. Joe Laurie, Jr." five times.

So Joe answered, "my name is Holbrook Blinn." The big man asked, "What have you done, Mr. Blinn?" Joe answered, "Six years ago, I was in the *Bad Man* for two years and for Mr. David Belasco I played the *Dove* for two years. The big man impatiently asked, "Yes, but what have you done for the last two years?"

"For the last two years," says Joe, "I've been dead you Son Of A Bitch!"

============

Al Kaye (now of Benton & Bowles) booked me into the Mastbaum Theatre in Philadelphia. I was surprised to find myself the headliner, following Eddie Cantor, the Marx Brothers, Joe E. Brown, Marie Dressler, Fannie Brice and others. None of these people got less than ten thousand a week and I was following them at twenty-two fifty. Marie had the record for business; now what were they expecting of a "smallie" like me?

Al Kaye and Bill Goldman explained that it was Holy Week and didn't want to blow too much money, so booked me for cheap and a stinko picture—cheap when you consider the others' salaries. Thank heavens they weren't going to blame me for the bad business!

Opening day we break the record for the joint and no one can understand it. They figured out some excuse but were sure that tomorrow we'd fall on our cans. We kept breaking records every day I was there. This is preposterous, they say, but the dough is in the till. Goldman figures to find out if it *is* me and books me into the Earl Theatre the next week a few blocks away and I do the same kind of business.

Now he gets a great idea and I am so glad he thought of it. After closing at the Earl, he books me into six to ten theatres a day, doing a matinee and night show in each.

The routine is to drive up to a theatre at one p.m., stop the picture, do five minutes and drive to the next about one twenty-five and so on until about five thirty. The routine started again at seven and went on for six days. We must have played pretty nearly forty theatres.

For this I got a percentage of the business over the average eighteen week period and I wound up getting quite a bundle for myself.

============

On a Bill in San Francisco were Joe Frisco, Pat Henning, Three Stanley Brothers, and some gals. I did five shows a day and knocked out jokes in between, eating in the dressing room. Dead tired and to bed every night. But I felt pretty good one night and decided to go to the Bal Tabarin with Lucille Ball, who was in San Francisco doing some location scenes. Mr. Martinelli wanted to seat us at a front table, but we were not there for exhibitionism, just some food and quiet music.

The floor show started without comics; Lucille and I weren't too interested. We had plenty of laughs at the table. Then a dark-haired kid stepped out on the floor. She started to dance and Lucille and I swapped quick glances. They meant, "This kid is great!" The applause at the finish proved that the audience was reading our minds.

While she was doing the next number, I told Lucille I was going to send for the kid. Then I got scared of something that always stops me from talking to girls. You say "Hollywood" and they think it is strictly a make routine. I told her what I was thinking and Lucille said, "I'll send for her and then you talk."

The show over, she came to the table with her mother. We introduced ourselves and explained we wanted to recommend her for a test. Of course they were happy with the thought and while Lucille ordered them some food, I called and awakened Sam Briskin. After my description of the dancing, legs, bazooms and youth, he told me to sign her to an agreement in lieu of the regulation studio contract.

Next day she had her contract. Next week she was in Hollywood, made a test and had a real contract. Ann Miller has done well ever since.

Son and father

Saranac Lake, N.Y. Participating in William Morris' great charities, Peter Van Steeden, Ruth Morris, security officer, President Calvin Coolidge, Paul Whiteman and BR.

BR with Herb Shriner

Frank Morgan and BR

BR with Max Baer

How to Succeed in the Show Business

BY

BEN RUBIN

BUNK

BY

BENNY RUBIN

XXXX

OH, HOW

BULL-ETIN

BY

BEN RUBIN

Al Schacht and BR

BR with Louise Fazenda

Benny Fields and BR

BR with Bert Lahr

BR and agent for the stars Al Melnick, with Brod Crawford

BR, Jack Eigen and Milton Berle watch pest being removed from Copa Lounge, N.Y.

Joan Bennett, Tay Garnett and BR.

Dorothy Lamour and BR

BR, Lawrence Gray, Walter Catlett, Marion Davies and Charles Chaplin

BR, Irving Berlin, Norma Shearer and Irving Thalberg

Ladies of the Ensemble, Harry Ruby, Jack Haley and BR

BR, George Jessel and lovely models

BR and Tom Dugan

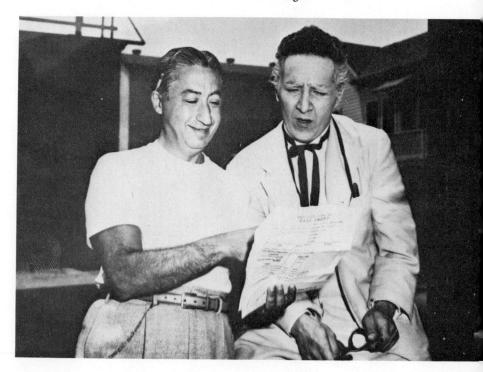

BR and Kenny Delmar

The Ritz Brothers, the Lombardos, the Rubins and the Gaines

Lilyan Tashman, BR and Louise Fazenda

Harry Langdon and BR 1922

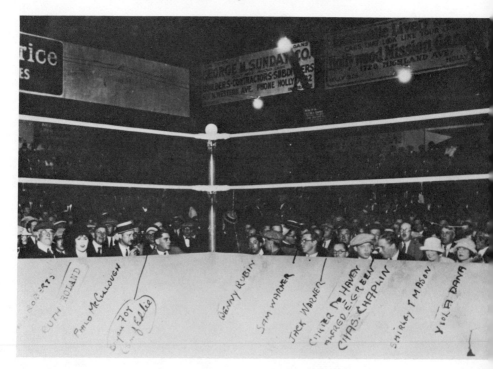

Ringside Hollywood Legion Stadium 1921

This is a Stickup, man?

Zeppo, Groucho, Chico, Gummo, Harpo

Happy Felton, Hal LeRoy, Mitzi Green and BR

Bugs Baer, BR, H.B. Warner and Bobby Clark

BR and Carole Lombard

Lou Costello, BR and Bud Abbott

BR and Wesley Barry

At the Palace, N.Y. with Grace Hayes

Jack Benny was prematurely gray

Mr. Costello, Jimmy Gleason, Bob Montgomery and BR in "Here Comes Mr. Jordon"

BR and Buster Collier, representing 1930, to the famous old timers, (left to right): De Wolff Hopper, Josephine Sabel, Louis Mann, Marie Dressler, William Collier, Fay Templeton, Lew Fields, Joe Weber and Barney Fagan. A scene in MGM review "The March of Time."

Buster Collier Jr., Betty Healy, BR and beautiful police lady

Joan Crawford and BR

Tells all. Man on right is Mike Stokey

BR and Polly Moran

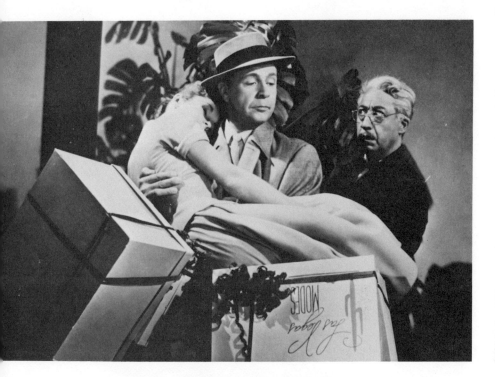

Debbie Reynolds, Dick Powell and BR

Leo G. Carroll, BR, Lee Patrick and John Banner

BR, Karl Dane, Gus Shy

Gus Van, Mary Doran, Tom Dugan, Joe Schenk, Wheezer Dell (Brooklyn Dodger Pitcher),B

Cliff Edwards, BR, Karl Dane and gentlemen

Harry Seymour (actor), Ray French (baseball player), Joe Schenk, Alfred E. Green, Gus V.
The visitors' wives and Colleen Moore

BR, Bessie Love, Frank Capra and Johnny Walker

BR. Make-up was the order of the day (1917-1918 burlesque)

George Douglas (burlesque comic), Jack Pearl, Harry Delmar, Harry Howard (vaude produc
Buddy Doyle (singer), Jimmy Hussay (Irish), best Jewish comic of the time. Picture was po
by Walter Winchell for his newly found career of columnist for N.V.A. News

BR and Bal Lloyd

Katherine Brown, Joe E. Brown, Eddie Cantor, Jack Benny, BR (top row)
Babe Marks (Mary's sister), George Burns, Ida Cantor, Gracie Allen, Mary Livingston

Bert Wheeler, Bill Woolsey, Milton Berle, Joe Penner, Victor Moore, BR

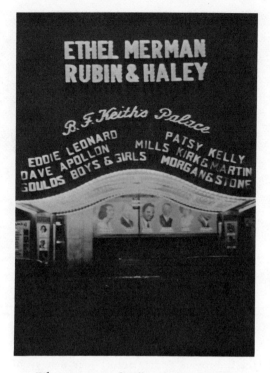

What every vaudevillian brags about

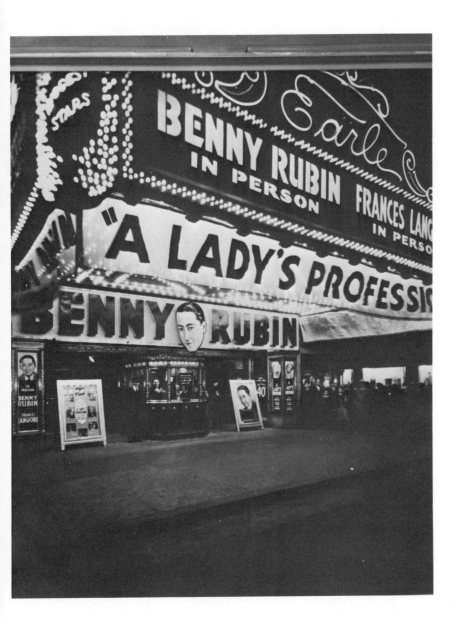

AL CAPONE AND SHOW BUSINESS

It was some time in 1929 when Jack Benny and I were under contract to MGM. I got an offer to do a radio show for "Orange Julius"—that is, if the *first* show was any good.

I fortified myself with Mary Livingston as a singer and comedienne. Our pianist was Dave Dryer. He wrote, "Ain't You Coming Out Tonight Cecilia?" and a lot of other song hits.

It was about ten minutes to air time. Jack was there and he was more nervous than we were. I wish he hadn't been, or he wouldn't have given me this lousy joke. He said, "In that Irish routine you do with Mary, have her ask you where you're from and you say, *Ireland,* Coney, Ireland."

Okay, the show started and I told a couple of the best jokes I knew.

Mary sang two songs.

We did the Irish routine with the Coney Ireland joke.

Dave Dryer played a short medley of hits, and I hate to tell you the truth, I don't remember what we did for a finish.

This much I *can* tell you, we were pretty happy with ourselves.

Ah ha, here comes the producer and the sponsor!

He spoke first to Dave, "Mister, maybe you wrote those songs, but you sure played them lousy." To Mary he said, "And you lady, you ain't no Sophie Tucker. And you! boy, do you stink, especially with that Coney Ireland joke."

Now the way I was brought up was to very politely hit the guy a belt in the mouth. I looked around, no Mary, no Dave, no Jack.

118

When I caught up with them in the parking lot, those three goons were laughing their heads off. And you know how Jack laughs! He was on the ground.

Okay, fade out. A few years later, there was a gang of us at the old Trocadero Cafe. Mary and I got up to dance. No sooner than we hit the floor, Mary said to me, there's a man waving at us and he's dancing our way. I looked and said, "Mary, would you like to have a glass of Orange Julius?" She mumbled something like, "Oh, no."

When the man and his lady sidled up to us, he said, "Remember me, Mr. Rubin?" I said, "Yes, one Orange Julius small." He gave me one of those prop laughs. I introduced Mary as Mrs. Jack Benny, but he didn't recognize her. Then he went into a rave about how great she was with Jack—and get this—he loved her singing. Mary charmingly said, "Thank you, Sir, you are very kind, but you know something? I ain't no Sophie Tucker!"

What the reaction from the guy was I'll never know. Mary and I were just learning to do the rhumba and we had enough trouble trying not to bump into everybody; when we told what happened to Jack, boom—there he was on the floor again.

=============

When I was acting in "Girl Crazy" in Chicago the men who were running the business end of the show kind of forgot to pay the actors. In fact, some of the chorus kids slept in the theatre. So I gave them an ultimatum on a Friday night, that I'd play the Saturday matinee and if the dough wasn't there for *all* of us I wouldn't go on the night performance. I had no understudy.

After the matinee on Saturday, a man came into my dressing room just as my dresser—one of the chorus boys—was helping me off with my clothes. He said, "Don't take nuttin off." I said, "Who the bleep are you?" He unfolded a switch blade knife and my dresser passed out, and one of his earrings fell off. I yelled, "Wait a minute, mister," and he yelled back, "*You* wait a minute. You said you wasn't goin on the show tonight and I'm here to see that you do, so don't take nuttin off!"

I said, "Look, guy, knife or no knife, my wife and daughter are expecting me for dinner and I'm going out through that door."

He said, "If you do, you'll go out with one ear."

Natch I didn't move. I put a cold towel to my dresser's face and revived him. Then I warned him not to tell anybody what was going on, and to bring me a sandwich and some coffee.

Well, anyway, I had my sandwich and coffee in the dressing room and did the evening performance. Before I left, the guy warned me he'd be back tomorrow and if I didn't show, he knew where my wife and kid lived.

After I squared myself away with my wife and daughter about what happened, I grabbed a cab and went down to the Metropole Hotel to see Al Capone.

You have no idea how tough it was to get to see him, but I had known him before he became a big shot. I was frisked in the lobby, while someone went to the phone and told Al I was there. Two guys escorted me to his suite on the top floor. After the amenities, I told him what happened.

When I explained the situation, he said, "I'll take care of it." I had a cup of coffee with him and left.

About five minutes before curtain time Sunday night, the guy with the knife was seated near me, when two well dressed men came into my dressing room. One said, "Is this the man who's going to cut your ear off?" The guy with the knife talked fast and loud, "I ain't gonna do nuttin to him, I'm onney trettenin him. I'm gettin a cee note to trettin him."

As dramatic as the situation was, I really broke up when the other visitor flashed a knife and said, "Don't you know, if you don't know how to cut a guy's ear off, you can give him blood poison?"

Boom! My dresser fainted again and this time both earrings fell off.

One of the two men picked up my dresser, slapped his face to bring him to and we left to go onstage. When I returned to my dressing room I looked for blood, bones—nothing. One of the box office men was waiting for me. Very quietly he said, "Here's all the money that's coming to you, will you count it and sign this receipt please?" I counted and signed. That's the whole story. Except I know you'd like to know what Capone had done to the trettner. This is the truth. The two guys put him on a plane to Canada; with this admonition . . . "You're giving Chicago a bad

120

name, now get ahdda here!"
Like they say—"That's show biz."

============

While playing in "Girl Crazy" in Chicago, a gentleman from MCA offered me a job in a night club that was to open in a week or so. It was murder to refuse a thousand dollars a week for two shows a night, but after being on the stage for two and a half hours (five on Wednesday and Saturday) I just had to turn it down.

An hour later, I got a call to meet Al Capone after the show at the Frolics Cafe. My wife and I went there and had supper with him.

He told me that Sam Hare and Joey Jacobson were good guys and good friends, and they needed me as their first attraction. "Al," I pleaded. "I'm tired and this thing will knock me out completely. If it was for you, it would be different." He said that it was for him, so I okayed it. The deal was for twenty-two hundred and fifty a week, one show a night. And to take up some time and pressure off me, he hired the Quartet from "Girl Crazy." The band was Irving Aaronson's Commanders. Once I opened, I did the two shows a night and had a wonderful time, all the time I was there.

Gregory Ratoff's show, "Wonder Boy" was closing in New York and I wanted to get back to California, so it was good for both of us that he played my part (we made the deal on the telephone).

A few days later, Ratoff came on and started to rehearse. During his visits to my dressing room, he sat in a big chair Texas Guinan had left there. It was wired under the seat and beneath my dressing table there was a pedal. I could step on this and the person in the seat would receive a shock. The chair was between the table and my trunk. When a person was contacted, he usually grabbed the table with one hand and the trunk with the other, for leverage to rise fast.

Ratoff sat with his overcoat rolled around his arms and his derby hat in his hands. So when he got the first shock, he couldn't grab anything and just bounced, crying, "Benechka, Benechka, something is biting me!" I assured him it was the nervousness of rehearsing that had him on edge. "What could possibly bite you?" He said, "I donyoh, but was biting me something!"

He sat down again and we worked at trying to get him not to pronounce the letter "L" in "folks." When I got him concentrating on my tongue and teeth for pronunciation, I really gave him a shot! He jumped a foot. I belted at him, "Look, Grisha, I can't help you if you're going to jump around." He yelled back, "I don't think so what it's nervuss, is someting in dat chair what is biting me in mine ass!"

I confessed that it was an electric chair. He said, "You are doing this to many people isn't?" I said, "Yes, and one of them was Al Capone." He smiled and said, "This is making me to love you. If is good enough for Al Capone is good enough for me."

============

If you were a devotee of Damon Runyon, you will recall his writing about a floating "crap game" in New York in the twenties. Or, you heard the character "Nathan Detroit" sing about it in *Guys and Dolls.* Or, if you were a guy like me, who in the twenties knew only two things, his vaudeville routine and the percentages of gambling odds, you know something of this dice-dealing enterprise.

Geography and instructions: First, you had to have the mentality to want to gamble and consort with the mob. And the mob then meant just that. No fancy lawyers running the rackets; it was merciless muscle and guns. Once accepted you got to know a man who at six p. m. would give you a street corner location. There, you met a second man, who would give you the exact address for the game that night. He regulated the traffic, so there would never be more than two people arrive at one time. At the door, you spoke a word given you by the last man and were allowed to enter.

The scene: Inside the loft, garage or spacious empty dining room, you saw a large table approximately ten by twenty. A large light hung over the table and just enough side lights to see around the rest of the room. Directly upstage center a man sat at the table with untold thousands in cash before him. He was the "house" man. To his right was the "stick" man, who controlled the dice and called the numbers when the dice stopped rolling. His eagle eye and timing of bets made told him when to return the dice to the shooter to roll again. To the left of the "house" man is one of many "floor" men who watch all of the action so there is no quarrel on payoffs.

This table did not have a mark on it in contrast to the dice table as you know it in Las Vegas. If you wanted to bet on "craps," "eleven," or the "hard" way, it had to be a bet made with an individual beside you.

All of this is set up nightly by expert crews of carpenters and electricians. The material is moved in a covered van and absolutely no one, except the controllers of this venture knew where the game would be, until six p. m. of the next day. The first two men who directed you never were told the exact address. A man called only "Baldy" represented the mob and Johnny Coakley, the protection.

Another sidelight of the room always contained two portable tables and chairs. On one was an assortment of sandwiches and cold drinks; there was not an established price, but no one ever gave the refreshment man less than a dollar.

At the other table, sat a man known as the "shylock." He would lend money on jewelry that he assessed with a discerning eye through a jeweler's loupe (eyepiece). If he knew you, he'd lend money at twenty percent, payable on a specific day set by him.

The house man's functions were to collect fifty cents for each shooter and cover any bet if you couldn't get the action from another player. He charged five percent for this service and you could bet him either way, win or lose. The only words he spoke all night were, "you're on," or, "no bet."

How you played the game: The stick man pushed the dice to you (after you've paid the fifty cents) and you rolled; the dice had to hit a wall of the table or it's not a shot. Another "no shot" is, if one or both of the dice went off the table.

When the die or dice have been retrieved, the stick man gives you new dice to roll, while a floor man scrutinizes the fallen cubes to see if someone had made a switch.

The shooter shoots, until he has thrown a number, (very seldom will a shooter make a bet on the come out), then the betting starts. You bet one another, unless, as I stated, if you couldn't get the action from a fellow player, you bet the house man.

If the number was ten and you are at the table, you both laid your cash in front of you like this: **T** for a ten. The reverse of ten is four, so you arranged your money like this: **⊥** . Five was: **V** and the reverse nine was: **∧** . Six was: **+** and eight was: **X** . Some big players brought playing cards 4, 5, 6, 8, 9, 10 and placed their money on the cards.

Since there was room for only a limited amount of players at the table, there would be fifty or sixty men who could not see the floor of the table, or the roll of the dice and they too would bet each other and rely on the voice of the stick man to call the numbers.

If you won a lot of money and had trepidations of being stuck up, a man would bodyguard you home for a price.

I was one of nine actors who were given the privilege of attending these sessions. Eight of us were conventional crap shooters and bet only to win. The ninth was also a "do" bettor, but had a different approach. He would arrive, wad a bunch of bills together, throw the lump over the heads of the players to the house man and holler: "They win for this." The house man merely said: "You're on, Lulu." If he lost, he left immediately, if he had a winner, the house man straightened out the crumbled bills and paid him. He would then stay and gamble.

This Lulu you knew as a member of the greatest trio in the entertainment business. But at the time of this yarn, he was doing a double act, Clayton and Edwards (Cliff Edwards). Later it was Clayton, Jackson and Durante.

On this particular night, "he won." The house man unscrambled a hundred and seventy five dollars and threw him three fifty. At six o'clock in the morning, a couple of us—who get broke early, but stayed to watch Lulu—escorted him to "Gerson's" for breakfast. This was the place that Lindy worked in as a waiter, before he had his own restaurants. After we had ordered our lox and eggs, we repaired to the men's room for an audit. He counted one hundred and twenty five thousand dollars.

He called his wife to join him immediately, placed the entire bundle on the seat of the commode and told us to take our best shot. We took the lox and eggs and stuck him with the check. He gave a one hundred dollar bill to the cashier and told him this was to take care of anyone who looked like they couldn't pay. (The cashier knew exactly who.)

We'll call his wife Chykee. As she came to the restaurant, Lulu gave her a bundle and she went home on a cloud.

Another vaudevillian won seventy five thousand. With the confidence he had of doing the same nightly, he went to the sixth floor of the Palace Building (where the theatre bookers dwelt), announced loud and clear that he understood his contract for twenty three weeks read: "pay or play," and threw them about four thousand dollars to cancel the contracts.

Exactly five days later, he was back and with a well modulated, kindly approach, asked for work. They gave him the twenty three weeks again, but nary a dime of the four grand.

Some unreliable or uninformed policemen crashed the game one night, grabbed all of the cash and ordered everybody to face the wall. Those that argued, or were too slow conforming were slugged. Next to me, with outstretched arms on the wall, was a former boxing champion, who was not popular with the police. When a cop yelled out the boxer's name and told him to turn around, he quickly grabbed a palm full of blood from another on the wall, smeared his face with it and turned around. The cop seeing the blood figured he had been beaten enough. (The boxer's name was Abe Attel.)

Other than Lulu's winnings, the most pleasant memory of this game was watching Nick the Greek lose about seven hundred thousand dollars. No, no, not the losing part of it, but this.

He went to the refreshment table, unwrapped a sandwich and drank from a bottle of Doctor Brown's celery tonic. Reaching into his pocket, he came up with twenty one dollars; he gave the man eleven dollars for the food, sat down and played the Shylock a game of "casino" for ten dollars—he lost. The Shylock offered to loan him any amount of money without his usual percentage. Nick declined, walked over to a floor man and asked him to give the stick man a hundred dollar tip for him . . . "Sure, Nick" . . . "Thanks, Baldy."

Most actors are still alive and I do not know just how many of the following are around, so left their names out of my remembrances:

Johnny Coakley (Political contact man)
Baldy   ?   (Chief floor man)
George McManus (they claim he killed Arnold
                    Rothstein)
Nickolas Dondolas (Nick the Greek)
Nigger Nate (Nate Bernstein from Portland, Oregon)
Big Augie
Little Augie
Big Frenchy
Larry Faye
Arnold Rothstein
Legs Diamond
Bill Duffy
Abe Attel
Nicky Arnstein
Butch Tower
Meyer Boston
Frank Costello
Anastasia Brothers
"Longie" Zwerling (Newark)
Muggsy Taylor
Lucky Luciano
Jimmy Kelly

MY INTRODUCTION TO HOLLYWOOD

Hollywood introduced itself to me in nineteen twenty, when I played the Original Orpheum Theatre in Los Angeles.

My act got third billing to Sophie Tucker and Paul Whiteman, yet it was my first time here and nobody knew me. Other acts had been here before and, of course, the big shots knew Sophie and Paul.

After the night show of the first day, I was on my way to "Coffee Dans," to see who I might kibbitz with and possibly see some movie stars. Standing near the stage entrance was a leading man I had seen many times. I figured he was waiting to see someone on the bill. He shocked the hell out of me by calling my name. Hey, what you know, I knew a star!

I complimented him on a couple of pictures I had seen him in and with his head kind of lowered he explained he was hustling ads for a theatrical newspaper. The wind-up was, I took a small ad and he went with me to Coffee Dans. While he was eating ham and eggs (I had lox and eggs) I learned of Hollywood's cardinal sin. He had committed it. He made two flops in a row and was labeled a loser.

Now dig this. At the same time there were two murders in the Colony, an actor was arrested for bigamy, another was involved in a hit and run accident, a well-known personage had fathered a child by a teen-age girl and emblazoned in the headlines was a story of an orgy involving six luminaries. Not one of them blew their jobs or standing in the community.

Oh, yeah, how about the actor who was on location in Mexico? This guy, loaded with Tequila, walked out onto the balcony of his suite and reviewed a passing parade. He didn't just review it, he gave his analysis. Of course he was arrested and paid a fifty dollar fine.

The injustice of failure still prevails. An actor or director makes a couple of stinkers and they are marked lousy. Neither the producer nor writer of those pictures suffers these indignities.

The producer puts the blame on bad direction or the artists not cooperating. He doesn't take a shot at the writer because he'd look bad for having accepted the story. He goes on to his next production.

The writer has a little the best of it. He can blame the producer for changing his story, the director for putting it on the screen badly and the actors for not portraying the parts as he wrote them. He just goes on to his next assignment.

The Broadway producer enjoys the same privileges. After the flop, when he gets through blaming the director and actors, he uses his other plus. These lousy critics. Angels are plentiful, so he just prepares his next show.

Take the case of Theresa Twirvv. The news media knock her brains out for leaving her husband and children for the director from South Malaguennia. Then *Variety* says, "Tondelayo smash at box office." She goes on to her next picture at triple the dough.

Now comes Timothy Tranafats, the "Prince of Pix." Five hits in a row and then bang! two flops. I stood behind him the other day in the unemployment line.

This castration does not happen in so-called legitimate business. A person has a bad season or even goes bankrupt and the people in his own business (sometimes competitors) come to his rescue. For having had a bad break, he is not banned from his livelihood.

Paradoxically, the best examples of helping a guy in your own business is practiced by gamblers. A man can have a run of bad luck (not just two failures) and presto there is new money.

The fact that a man has erred in his judgment, or the breaks went against him, does not change the fulcrum of the scales of chance. Without begging, signing notes, or putting up collateral, his contemporaries bankroll him.

Not so in my racket. Two strikes and you're out. What would have happened to Willie Mays if a Hollywood mogul managed the Giants instead of Leo Durocher? Twenty eight times at bat (one hundred and twelve swings) without a hit.

Like Sidney Skolsky says, "But I love Hollywood." Yet, don't you dare make a mistake! The saddest commentary on this subject happened to Al Jolson. Oh, I know you saw the movie, but you couldn't feel pain as I did.

We had ranches a street apart. During a happy dinner, playing bridge, at the fights and even between races at the track, he'd get a faraway look in his eyes. My vision of what he was looking at was a picture of a guy in overalls taking his name off the marquee.

Two bad pictures and they wouldn't even invite him to play a benefit. Now who the hell were the "they?" One guy who was a director only because his nephew hired him. Another guy who was only interested in the receipts and a third man who considered him passe.

Because it was his club and his wife had given a gang of money for the tickets, he condescended to attend.

The show went on and on (with some people who couldn't carry his shoes) and at the end of the thing, one of those three nothing people thought it would be nice to honor him by allowing him to take a bow.

The audience stood en masse for his ovation and a clamor started, "We want Jolson, we want Jolson!"

The rest you know. Without his own accompanist and no rehearsal he made everybody in the joint look like midgets.

It was the same Sidney Skolsky that got the idea and produced the *Jolson Story*.

That same week I ran into a man I had seen pitch a one hitter for the San Francisco "Seals" against the Portland "Beavers." You knew him as Alfred E. Green, the famed director. You also must have heard of another director by the name of Benny Stoloff. Benny played second base for Portland and was the guy who spoiled Al's no hitter.

Al and his wife, Vivian, took me to the class nite club of Hollywood—at the time—"The Little Club," (upstairs next door to the Roosevelt Hotel). Man, did I see stars! Mary Pickford with Owen Moore, Jack Pickford with Marie Prevost, Wally Beery and his bride Gloria Swanson. There was Charlie Chaplin with Edna Purviance and Sid Grauman and a stag table with Fatty Arbuckle,

Buster Keaton, Snitz Edwards and Slim Summerville.

I was shocked to see Ernest Torrance cutting up touches with Richard Barthelmess. Only a few days before, I had seen a movie where Torrance buried the heel of his boot in Barthelmess's face. (I think it was *Intolerance.*)

Fatty Arbuckle took over the drums from Abe Lyman for a dancing session.

Vivian saw my eyes bulge in wonderment and invited me to dance, so I could get closeup views of the stars. I was strictly a hoofer and knew from nothing when it came to ballroom dancing. I knew that a time step was followed by a break (dance step) and at the end of every eight bars, another break and change steps. It must have been murder for Vivian, but she gave no sign of discomfort.

I must have halted with a jerk when I came within two feet of my favorite movie star, Ruth Roland. Vivian sensed it and a few dances later, there I was, dancing within a foot of my Queen. (If you've ever seen Ruth Roland close up, it had to be a foot.) She dug my hoofing style and all of a sudden, the floor was cleared and there we were, just the two of us. Yeah, yeh, we were a hell of a hit and I was in heaven.

What followed is too long a yarn, so I'll lay it on you fast. She got me a test at Fox and I blew a contract with a stupid ad lib. Sol Wurtzel offered me a contract if I would have my nose bobbed. My stupid answer was, "I won't cut off my nose to spite my race."

Some vaudevillians went for the nose job and got contracts. Irving Cummings, Ben Bard, Lew Brice and Georgie Stone.

Later there was Fannie Brice, Milton Berle, Bea Benadaret, Jan Murray and Dean Martin.

Tony Bennett, full treatment, face lift, nose and teeth.

Nose and hairline, Berle.

Hair transplants, Sinatra and Bishop.

Nose and chin, John Conte.

Ears pinned back, literally, Raft, Gable and Crosby.

There's a flock of them that wear hairpieces, but George Burns' is the only one that is perfect.

Jessel has a full complement. Dark brown for evening wear and TV. Dark brown with gray at the temples for funeral orations. Mixed brown and gray for business meetings. Doesn't wear any when he's entertaining the Armed Forces.

Jerry Colonna's answer to people who ask, "Is your mustache real?" "No, it's a phony, the real one is here in my pocket." (He shows them a phony mustache.)

Durante's nose is his trademark. Bob Hope exploits his for jokes. Danny Thomas and Danny Kaye were both asked to have alterations. Thomas answered, "This is me, take it or leave it." Kaye told them to go to hell! What Barbra Streisand told them, I don't think they did. "I don't know of anyone who was ever able to accomplish that feat."

WILLIAM MORRIS

Mr. William Morris was the most wonderful man I had ever met in my life. I'm as wary of superlatives as the next guy, but with regard to Mr. Morris I'm pulling out all the plugs. He was, and will always be Mr. Good, Mr. Nice, and Mr. Charity.

Mr. Morris was doing another of his celebrated shows at Saranac for charity. Up to this time I had played as many benefits as anyone around, considering my years in the game; some Sunday nights I had raced around like mad and managed to work in three such dates. But the Saranac thing was the one everybody in the business wanted to play—and I hadn't been asked. Year after year I awaited the honor, and it finally came.

I don't remember the entire show, but some of the participants were Arthur (Bugs) Baer, Tyrone Power, Sr., and Ben Bernie, the old Maestro, and his band. It was a smooth presentation all the way, and to everybody's delight Mr. Morris again made a lot of money for charity. More important than all that to me was the fact that I got acquainted with the entire Morris family as well as probably the smartest fellow I had ever met, Abe Lastfogel. He had come to the Morris office as an office boy a few years before. While Mr. Morris was ill, he'd built up a pretty good business.

In rapid succession he got me a few days work, replenished the bankroll—and rolled over from his side of his bed to make room for me. His sister, Bessie, was a career girl, but got home early enough to cook for us. Abe was alone in the office, in the Putnam Building (now the Paramount, or whatever they are calling it). He got Harry Lanetska, an Orpheum booker, to join the office. Harry brought in Frances Arms, a terrific singing gal with many dialects. Because we both could do all the accents we were a bit hit around the office.

Lanetska then brought in a blackface comic who played music on an iron pipe. His name was Bob Burns.

Meanwhile it was time for another show at Saranac. Mr. Morris had me come up a month earlier and live in the house built for Harry Lauder. It was called the "Wee House."

I slept in the Wee House, but ate in the big house. Mrs. Morris was a charming hostess and very dignified. There was lovable Aunt Ella, daughter Ruth, and Bill Jr. who was in town. Up to now, the actors came up a day ahead, visited hospitals and did the show. Of course, they were entertained royally by the Morrises.

This time we did things differently. One morning Abe Lastfogel, Bill Morris, Jr., Benny Thau, Harry Lanetska, Abe Myers and Eddie Elkins came up and the gang of us (except Bill) slept in the Wee House. That afternoon the Wee House gang ran out and ruined a golf course.

After dinner that evening the motley ensemble went to a swank hotel in nearby Lake Placid. While I put on a show in the dining room, my roommates helped sell tickets. I'd tell a few gags and start off the floor. When the audience applauded for more, the condition was to drop money in the boys' hats. I'd do another few minutes and quit. They yelled for me to dance and I'd ask for dough for that. We had a good evening of collecting for the charity show.

Mr. Morris had raised the money to build a Catholic Church and these funds were to maintain it. Later on, another show paid off the mortgage. Mr. Morris had done this for years for every kind of a charity for every nationality where money was needed. It was just about this time that Mr. Morris conceived the idea of the Jewish Theatrical Guild. He spoke a line out of his heart one night, and the Guild has used it as a guiding slogan ever since. The line was: "We take from our own and serve humanity."

The next day, up came Paul Whiteman, Harry Fender (Ziegfeld Follies), and Abe Goldstein, world's featherweight champion. That evening we went to a different hotel to sell tickets. Again I did the gag routine and picked up a few bucks. Then I said something about introducing a star that got ten thousand dollars a week for appearances, but wouldn't bring him on unless we got more money. Abe, Benny, Lanetska, Elkins and Myers collected another gob and I brought on Paul Whiteman. They cheered and, of course, wanted him to play. We charged them twenty-five dollars a couple to dance to Whiteman's fiddle and the little orchestra there. The leader's name was Peter Van Steeden. He was present, I know, because I have a picture of us shaking hands with President Coolidge.

For the next intro I wanted more dough because the gent usually got fifty thousand or more for an appearance. The people shelled out and the Wee House gang nabbed every buck in sight. I brought on Abe Attel Goldstein, the champion, to a terrific ovation. Now—did the folks want him to box? They yelled that they did. More money! We brought with us two pairs of twelve-ounce boxing gloves and rehearsed Harry Fender singing a waltz, while we did a clowning boxing act. After a few laughs, a young Cornell college student walked on the floor. Clad in dinner jacket and wearing horn-rimmed glasses. He announced.

"Pardon me, gentlemen. My name is Joe Lazarus, and if I can, I'd like to help with your entertainment." We stopped and asked him if he sang or danced. He replied, "Neither. I am the amateur featherweight champion of the world and would box Mr. Goldstein if it would enhance the show."

I looked at Abe and he nodded. While Lazarus was taking off his coat, dress collar and tie, I told the audience of the whispered dialogue and the match. They cheered. Lazarus then turned to the audience and said, "But for a lot more money—how about it, Dad?" His Pa had already given about five hundred and came up with another grand. The Wee House boys were running from table to table, gathering the folding stuff and cramming their hats full.

Okay, I announce the bout—they start. Abe plays with the guy for a minute or so and then gets stung with two corking left jabs. He smiles. Two more catch him on the nose and we can see that he's starting to burn. He moves around Lazarus' left hand and puts in a couple of his own. I start to fret; the thing is becoming serious. Lazarus jabs Abe with a left; when he starts another, Abe lets go with the right hand that made him champion. Lazarus just moves a bit to the right, lets the punch go over his shoulder and hits Abe with the prettiest left hook since Charlie White. I hit the cymbal near the drums, call the bout a draw, and, shaking hands with Lazarus (but pushing him all the way), never let go until he is safely at his table. The Wee House boys got Abe out of there and we don't breathe easily till we are sorting the loot on Lanetska's bed.

Clayton and Jackson had just added a piano player to their act, by the name of Jimmy Durante.

When the trio arrived, they first wanted to go hospital visiting. The usual routine is to go bed-to-bed and cheer people. These guys sang, clowned and emptied their pockets of money to be split up in a ward. Then sent to New York for more and did it everywhere they went.

With them came a kid that Abe had picked up in New York. He was a good hoofer and could make you laugh when he danced. I was a little jealous because comedy dancing was my forte. This guy killed the people; he's been doing it ever since. I worked with this Ben Blue later when he owned half of Slapsie Maxie's in Los Angeles!

That night in the Wee House, the boys got hungry about midnight. What to do? We couldn't go to the big house that late and wake everyone with our prowling. The only way out we had was to go to town. It was miles to walk, and cold. Then someone came up with the bright idea of stealing the family car. Only two of us knew how to drive and we drew straws. I lost. Then we drew again to see which one of the non-drivers was going to go with me. Abe Myers was it.

We bundled up and sneaked into the pitch blackness. Got to the garage, silently opened the door, but you can't start a motor silently. We started to push it down the road a piece and almost pushed it into the lake. I started the motor—it sputtered and died. Just then we heard Aunt Ella's voice ring out, "Stop or I'll shoot!"

Quickly we got out of the car, identified ourselves in loud whispers and told her where we were going. Ella gave us the okay and we ate that night. Next night when we came from hustling hotels, there was a tray of food that high in the Wee House.

MAX BAER AND I

While doing an act with Max Baer when he was the heavy-weight champion of the world, Max got an invitation to spend the weekend at Mrs. W. R. Hearst's home on Sands Point, Long Island. He was overjoyed, but Ancil Hoffman, his manager, refused to go with him. He appealed to Jack Dempsey, but Jack, who had never been in any kind of a fight outside of a ring, feared Max's playful temper might get him in some kind of a jam and naturally he'd be forced to become involved, so he begged off. Max was beside himself and threatened all kinds of things. Then Mrs. Hoffman took me to one side and said, "Look, Benny, this boy thinks that mingling with society is greater than being champion. Let him have his pleasure. Not only that, but he'll listen to you and that will keep him out of trouble." She sold me. I invited myself and he accepted but warned me not to try to top him. We packed sport clothes, but wore dinner jackets that Saturday evening. Mine was the conventional black tie. Max wore a white mess jacket. You know what his shoulders looked like when he was in shape. Now add padding, yet! He looked like he had a midget on each shoulder.

A long limousine picked us up. Two men jumped out of the car and took our bags. Max asked me why two guys? I told him one was the footman. He bumped me hard with his elbow. We got into the tonneau and Max asked again, why two men? I rolled up the glass partition and explained again; one was the chaffeur, the other the footman.

Max rolled down the glass and tapped the second man's shoulder.

"Hey, Bud, what are you—the co-pilot?" The man stiffly answered, "No, Sir, I am the footman!" Max rolled the glass up again and said angrily, "You told him to say it! And if you pull anything on me like that with these society people and make a sucker out of me you'll be sorry." I said, "Okay, you call him co-pilot from now on, enjoy."

In front of this miniature castle my stomach does a flip. What am *I* doing here? Nobody asked me to come; they want the champ! And they don't really want him either—just the title, not the man. The co-pilots take our bags and are gone.

Taking a deep breath, I prepare for the ordeal. Max takes the steps two at a time, all fifty or more, then hollers, "Come on." I shush him and he says, "Don't shush me! I can't stand to be shushed, especially in front of people. And please, please help me be a big man in there. Okay?" I echo, "Okay."

He pressed the buzzer. The liveried butler opened the door. Max said, "Hi, pardner, gimme five," and extended his hand. The butler backed off and said, "This way, please." We were butlered into a drawing room.

Max said, "What the hell's the matter with him? Everybody else wants to say "hello" or get an autograph, and that bum refuses to shake hands with me." "Listen, Max," I said, "this guy is a butler and it is not proper for a servant to shake hands with a guest, see?" Max said, "I don't see nothin'. Does he make more money than a champ?" Then he started bouncing on a very thick, expensive carpeting. "Hey, you could get knocked on your can on this thing and bounce right up." I said, "Max, please don't—," but that's as far as I got. "You lousy comedian, will you leave me alone and quit lecturing me?"

At that moment Mrs. Hearst arrived. She was very charming. More people arrived. I got a few fast "hellos," and in a little while there was a circle around Max, with me on the fringe. Finally, I took myself to a nook way over there and was admiring the many murals, or are they paintings? All of a sudden, a face I knew excited me. Do I know anybody in society? Oh, sure, that's Jay O'Brien, who was a tobogganer in the Winter Olympic Games. But he wouldn't remember me. He was introduced to Max, just as Max was looking at me with a twinkle, as much as to say, "How'm I doing?"

O'Brien caught the by-play, looked over at me and called my name loudly. I was surprised and delighted that he'd remembered me. Over he came and told me a funny story. I told him one and he howled. A few of Max's customers turned to look our way. One of them walked to us. She was a gorgeous woman and seemed to float over that rich rug. Jay introduced me to his charming wife, Dolly Fleischmann . . . yeh, yeh, from the yeast.

Jay had me repeat the story. She laughed and called to a few of her friends. That's all I needed. When Max lost a few listeners, you could see the veins in his forehead and neck stick out a foot. Thank heavens, we were in polite company, or you'd be calling me Pugnose.

Though I was holding my own, I edged the group back to Maxel. Dames is dames, society or otherwise, and they ooh'd and ah'd, all over his muscles. He made me his pal, by putting his arms around my shoulders. To the four hundred, it was affection. To me it was bone crushing time in Dixie, he was getting even with me!

Over the others' heads he could see the entrance to the room. His eyes narrowed to a very interesting "look at this babe!" Under his breath he asked me her name. Luckily, I remembered her face from newspaper pictures with thoroughbred horses. I whispered fast, "Isabel Dodge Sloan; she owns Cavalcade." Max grinned. "Watch this." After the introduction he said, "Miss Sloan, I saw your movie three times." She asked, "Movie? What movie?" Max replied, "Cavalcade. You made Cavalcade, didn't you?" She answered, "I've never made a movie, but I own a horse named Cavalcade." Max reached for me, but I had sneaked away the minute he said, "I saw your movie." You should have seen the silly look on his kisser.

I stayed far away from Max at dinner, desiring no contact with him whatsoever. He sat opposite Mrs. Hearst and a sleeper jump from me. Near me were Mrs. Rhinelander Stewart, Mrs. William G. McAdoo, Jr., and a beautiful lady whose name was Ryan, married to a member of the Thomas Fortune Ryan clan.

For thirty-five years I had not dropped my dinner in my lap or had a piece of fish adorn my lapels. Tonight, of all nights, I was as timid as a rabbit lest I do anything to mar my entrance into society. The service was solid gold and each utensil (there were seven thousand kinds of every plate) had a carved figure on it. I watched the others pick up their gold tools, one at a time. No mistakes so far; no crabmeat on my shirt front. Then, from far out there in right field, Max yelled at me, "Hey, Rubin, get a load of the gold statues on the silverware!" I didn't answer or dare look into the faces around me.

One monoclad guy by the name of "Nino" had a mouthful and he laughed it right out of his mouth. Where did it land? Just call me "Show One Cuff" Rubin. A lady to my right (not the lovely Ryan gal) said, "Isn't he horrible! His manners, his English! What do they see in him? He is just a beast that goes about beating men to the earth. Gad, I cawn't stand him!"

Some of the other British-speaking New Yorkers defended Max. I said nothing. Then the same gal who worried about Max's manners and English turned to me and told the filthiest story I'd ever heard. I wanted to hit her a "backhander," but I did nothing. Even with my background I haven't got the answer for that Park Avenue pig. There were more such sallies around this alley and dinner was finished. There was a bit of society style kibitzing while they sipped a sweet schnapps in the salon and then came movies. (Not Cavalcade.) The projection room had a lavender light, facing away from the screen; it didn't hurt the picture, but the customers could see the champagne brought in by the trayload. The high class people talked all the way through the picture. *Variety* would have said, "Society and propriety, but no sobriety."

After the movie, the men started card games and Maxie boy got himself a bevy of gals around him. Jay and his lovely Dolly took me for a stroll around the grounds. We saw beautiful landscaping, outdoor tennis courts, indoor courts, guest houses, and the beautiful view of the water.

At bedtime Mrs. Hearst, who had left us strictly alone to have fun where we found it, asked what we wanted for breakfast, and which morning papers. Was she kidding? We asked for the Hearst papers. Then as a gag, I asked for the *Daily Forward* and, sure enough, there it was the next morning.

Lying there between those satin sheets, it frustrated my little mind that this was the second time in my life that I'd been in the company of more than three people without being called on to do a show. I went to sleep with my jokes intact.

The next day I spend with Jay O'Brien, cutting up touches about the Winter Olympics, watching tennis games and early to bed. I saw the lovely brute once at dinner and not again until we pushed off with the co-pilots in the morning. Max rolled up the glass in the car and asked, "You didn't know that after you went to bed Saturday night, I got up again?" "No." He continued, "You didn't see me all day Sunday, or Sunday night either, did you?" "No." Then he grins and puts up more fingers than the guy in the show, *Mr. Roberts.*

I MADE A KING LAUGH

No comic will ever again be afforded this honor with this particular kind of king because there will never be another San Simeon!

Well, maybe if some totalitarian force takes over our country, and even then, no comic will be invited, because who will dare to laugh?

My king didn't wear a crown, medals, or a ribbon across his chest, yet he was monarch of everything he surveyed.

He didn't whack you over the shoulder with a sword and make you a knight. He belted you with the printed word and it was up to you as to which way you wanted to fly.

Wouldn't you give the monicker "King" to a man who owned a string of newspapers, thousands of acres of land all over the world, priceless objects of art, a palace and at least a hundred bucks in his pocket at all times?

He would never throw his weight around with little people, but he'd belt Presidents, real Kings and the big shots of industry.

The king I made laugh was Mr. William Randolph Hearst. Not Junior—Senior. It was always easy for comics to make Junior laugh, he wakes up laughing.

Because of my kind of nutty humor, Mr. Hearst invited me to the Shangri-La for a month. It wasn't just splendiferous, or luxurious. It was the most! The livin' end!

Before I get into the meat of the yarn, here is just an hors d'oeuvre.

Picture a guy who was brought up to sleep on two chairs in the winter and a fire escape in the summer, getting into a bed that was indented with the groovy curves of the Marquise de Pompadour? It was a double bed and I doubled sleeping on one side, then the other, trying to guess which side the chick slept on. What a pad!

Dig this! I sat on the throne which graced the form of Katherine (the something) and in wonderment contemplated one great shock to my nervous system—discovered that one of them was a bidet. What did I know from bidets? To me it was a two-holer.

That was for openers—now we go back to the beginning.

It's September of 1929 when I am lucky enough to be six weeks into a picture with Marion Davies, when they could have knocked me off in two.

One day Marion good morning'd us with "Who'll join me in a bit of breakfast?" We joined her—sixty three of us. The cost of the groceries, plus the time consumed, could have bought a small house with three bidets.

When everyone was wiping the eggs off their mouths, in came a truckload of gifts for everybody. When she saw the eyes pop she quickly said, "No, no, this is not the wrap-up of the picture, relax. It's just that I'm tired and I'm going up to the ranch (a ranch she called it) for a month. We'll finish this turkey when I come back." Now, about these gifts that were handed out. A lot of research must have been done by Billie Williams (Marion's right arm) because nobody got nothin' they didn't need.

I'll clue you in on something only a few of Marion's closest friends knew. It didn't have to be your birthday or Christmas for her to send you something. Little things like a home, completely furnished with a car in the garage.

Not just beds in hospitals—wings. You should have as many years of good health as the number of mortgages that were paid off on homes and churches. Anonymously!

Okay, so I am invited to California's heaven. Could be you've been to San Simeon, maybe you read about it, but not the way it was seen by a comic's eyes.

Ready? . . . Okay, come on, I'll take you up there.

On the private train there were more than a hundred well known people, but I'll just mention a few I liked most. Jane Peters, later Carole Lombard; Connie Bennett, Ann Pennington,

Cliff Edwards, Dorothy Mackail, Eileen Percy, Barney Glazer, Mary Eaton, Millard Webb. A standout was a Washington, D. C. newspaper publisher who I remember vividly as one of the most devout bottle men I ever met.

The groceries and service on that train, of course, was the most! The wine and liquor flowed copiously, but since I don't drink I cannot report on the vintages. These celebrities were patsies in card games, and I won a few bucks from them without cheating; the card sense and psychology I learned from a misspent youth was sufficient. When I retired to my drawing room I found it had three beds in it—all for me.

In the morning it was breakfast in the diner or in your room, just as m'lord desired. Detraining, we were greeted by a large convoy of chauffeur-driven limousines. We bowled along for about ten miles or so to the ranch.

What a grand entrance! There are guards to identify everybody, then you start to drive a long way to the castle. You pass a herd of gnus, camels, and I don't remember what else, except no lions. But wait a minute. There are lions—a flock of them, right on the road. The women scream and the men grit their teeth. However, when we get up close, it's an optical illusion. The lions are there all right, but a moat protects the road at a sharp turn. The lions can't get across. Big joke: I hollered louder than the women.

There are more animals in groups, but I am too scared to notice what they are. On both sides of the road are huge cases and crates, hundreds of them. This is no double talk; a real castle that my king bought somewhere in Europe. Now, I've seen them move houses on rollers, but how do you move a castle across land and ocean then on land again to this joint? Very easy. It's so simple that even you can do it. It'll be a little expensive, but here's the technique.

First you find the castle that you reach by camel or pogo stick and have enough loot to buy it. Then you build a railroad to the castle. Now you bring to the spot railroad cars for sleeping, eating, flat cars and of course an engine to pull the whole shmeer. In these cars are carpenters, architects, cooks and laborers. Also, every machine and tool for the "easy way" to move a castle.

First thing they do is to chop down trees, make them into

what it takes to build a sawmill. Then they chop down more trees, which are made into lumber suitable for crating. While this wood is drying, they dismantle the castle. This is no soft touch because the guys who put that thing up didn't use modern gadgets like nails, screws or gimmicks. They made iron things out of the ore in the ground and put this Motel for Monks up for keeps.

All right, so they do it. Now they crate the thing, move it on the flat cars to another railroad where it is transferred somehow to a ship. The ship comes to America and then by parcel post they ship it to where we see it now. Wouldn't it be funny if this is a whole made-up story? I don't think so, because the man who told it to me paid the tab. In fact, he had a couple of bucks left over.

Back at the ranch we arrive at the big castle already uncrated and right in the middle of nowhere, it's an inspiring sight. Our bags are grabbed by servants, and we are taken to our quarters. Cliff Edwards and I are in a cloister, way up in that corner up there, somewhere over the rainbow.

An elevator takes us up and the first thing we gander in the cloisters are twin poster beds that have steps leading up to them. Cliff and I are like two small boys, playing price. We make up jokes about what everything costs, and later find out that we were wrong. It cost more. We go down the elevator to see what a five cent newspaper will buy.

There are some three hundred and seventy-five thousand acres. The whole thing faces the Pacific Ocean and on a clear day you can see Istanbul. There's the castle I told you about (the un-packed one) with eight million rooms. I don't know how many private bungalows. They call them guest houses. Little joints with seven or eight rooms, replete with kitchen and loaded with groceries. The antiques, tapestries, paintings and furniture alone are worth at least four hundred million, give or take a buck.

Now come lanes, or walks. Maybe they're called promenades. Miles of them and every few feet are bigger-than-life marble statues of saints, kings, queens. Hundreds of them, and each one cost a zillion dollars. The swimming pools are lined with marble, each piece put in by hand mendel angelo and brought from Italy. I am not sure there wasn't gold in them there dunkers.

There is a tennis court, boat house, stables. The servants live in a small village all their own. There's a big storeroom where the guests can get swim suits, jodphurs (you know, stretch pants), tennis clothes, shoes, rackets, any size or color. There is a full zoo too.

As I recall the big house, you walked into a foyer bigger than your whole home, even if you own the biggest in your town. There was a card room (they called it a salon). There was a piano and organ in another nook. (Nook? The Yankee Stadium outfield.) This room was once a monastery in some far-off land. It too went through the castle-in-the-crate routine. On the ceiling in many squares, maybe 15 or 20, were carved images of saints. It was too beautiful for words. My kind of words, anyway. Outside of our cloister and Mr. Hearst's library, I didn't venture into any of the rest of the rooms.

Unlike most society clambakes, in this palace with my king and maid Marion, everyone is even-up. They don't read your clippings or count your money.

Since I had never been in society before, this was a brand new bit for me. The only time I was in this league was in Lake Placid where I broke bread with two big names you only see in Cholly Knickerbocker's column. Let's call them Mr. and Mrs. Richberch.

He was an Olympic tobogganer.

They clued me in on what makes you a blueblood. . . . An injection won't help. Her great great grandfather was a working stiff on the building of the first railroad; but because he could belt you out with one punch, he was made a foreman. After the two iron horses made their meet, they made him boss of a railroad yard.

He got his two sons jobs in the front office. They parlayed their salaries into stock in the company. By the time they had kids (one was her father) they owned fifty percent of the joint, and were invited into society.

His story was about the same as hers, except his pure blueblood lines came from bricklayers. Yet, now a laborer, or a bricklayer can't get past the dogs at their back entrance. Now that I've smartened you up on how to be a blueblood, let's go back to the "Ranch."

One day W. R. took me to see a room that had a big machine in it, on which you could see an entire newspaper come up. He was pleased with my wonderment, then laughed when I asked for the baseball scores. He picked up a phone, and from that day till I left, I got all the ball scores . . . inning by inning.

Nothing was demanded of you except that you be on time for luncheon and dinner. Breakfast was on all morning. No one mentioned this, but I learned that you didn't leave the table until he did. The knives, forks, spoons, and so forth, all had beautiful carvings on them.

Then there were picnics. If you rode horses you rode; but if you were me, you went by car. The ride was long, beautiful and interesting. About every half mile there was a phone on a tree in case you got lost on this freeway of trees. At about twelve-thirty or so you came to a clearing in the woods, and there in front of you were chefs and waiters . . . serving more goodies than you'd find at Chasens. . . . All for free and you can't even tip.

In the evening there were the latest movies in the beautiful projection room. Wait a minute . . . that's too plebeian . . . the motion pictures were shown in the palatial "Cinema Salon." During the show, champagne was served. I had seltzer water (for two cents plain).

One night I was inveigled into a bridge game with Marion, Dorothy Mackail and Connie Bennett. When my partner was Marion or Dottie, I was okay, but when La Bennett started to bid in French, I was dead! The other gals brought her back to my mental capacity and I think I lost a buck and a half!

I'd never played tennis, and in the swimming pool I was a sneaker-in; so the only time I was really in my element was at the Pool Table. I beat Cliff out of a couple of ukeleles, and the owner of the Washington *Post* for a grand. Nice place for a hustler, San Simeon!

You'd have flipped if you could have seen Cliff and me gandering at the others at mealtime so we'd know what the scoop was, with what fork does one use for what? Should we try to eat from left to right like some were doing? I tried and got a hunk of fish in my lap. Cliff was more successful, because he cheated by using a spoon. There was the time when you're supposed to dig protocol. What would you do if a guy caught you spitting in the chalk cube in a pool game? Does one deny it? Do you give the guy his money back, or do you politely, gently and firmly butt him in the belly with your pool cue? I did neither. I logically proved to him that he must have done it accidentally. He believed me because he was stoned.

Here's what I brought back with me and I'll never forget it. Any time I get in a bind mentally, I close my eyes and relive that month at San Simeon. The memory of Marion's graciousness, Mr. Hearst's unobtrusiveness into your daily pleasures. Nothing was asked of you, nor was anything expected from you. Other than "Come, make yourself at home."

FEUDIN', FIGHTIN' & FUNNIN'

Returning from Europe on the *Berengeria* in 1934, I had a bit of a tiff. During the day, people played tennis and Sam Fischer swam in the ship's pool. In the neighborhood from which I sprang, there weren't any pools and we had hardly enough dough for bread, let alone tennis rackets; so I spent my time doing something that was a kid ambition. My mind was sure about this thing, my reflex muscles told me I was right, but somehow the two never could quite get together, which caused me pain and embarrassment many times; yet there I was, boxing with the instructor in the ship's gym. The evenings we spent with some nice people and on next to the last day out, Sam and I sat down at a small table in the magnificent room and listened to the beautiful music. About two tables away, a big guy we'll call the Vulgar Boatman, yelled over to us: "Hey, you two guys are Americans, come on over and have a drink with me." We thanked him and said no, so he brought his drinks over to our table. He said, "These lousy French and Englishmen won't talk to me because I am an American; they think I'm not good enough. I got more dough than any of them; I own ships of my own." His language was rough; we tried to ignore him. The big fellow said, "I think you stink like the rest of them. I just came from the only country that is run correctly, GERMANY. What they are doing over there, I am going to see that they do in America." I got up and so did Sam and we walked away. He tossed epithets after us.

The next day Fischer was in the pool. I was in the gym again when in walked this big guy and challenged me to a fight. I turned white and got sick to my stomach. The English boxing instructor told the man he was much too big for me and he tried to pacify him. With that, the big guy threw a sucker right-hand at me, and I hit him with a left hook "downtown," but way down, near the battery. When he doubled up, I threw my entire 140 pounds into an upper cut and then a straight right-hand with all the strength I had right on his chin like I always dreamed about and—out he went. I ran like hell to my stateroom, never bothering to remove my gym clothes, or boxing gloves. Sam unlaced my bloody gloves and snapped: "You could be thrown in the brig for this."

A few minutes later there was a knock and in came the purser and first mate. In very broad British the mate said, "Sir, we understand that you have had an altercation in the Jimnaazium!" I started to talk fast, but was interrupted. "We did not come here to complain, but to condone. That VULGAR BOATMAN has been a source of annoyance to passengers and us before. Is there any favor you would like granted?" I replied, "Thank you, gentlemen, and as long as you ask, how about having a radio to-night? We'd like to hear the Max Baer-Carnera fight for the heavy-weight championship." He mumbled something about interfering with the wireless. But, we got the radio.

I told Walter Winchell the story of my battle on the high seas. He said he had printed this guy's name before, along with some other haters, but people didn't believe all that he was writing about a lot of guys. They proved later to be what he said they were . . . We meet this guy again later so don't go away.

Half a dozen messages from Max Baer, Ancil Hoffman and Jack Dempsey awaited me at the St. Moritz. (How did they know we were arriving from Europe?) I called Baer to congratulate him and his answer was, "We've been looking all over for you, come right over to the Park Central Hotel."

In Max's suite were Ma and Pa Baer, Buddy, Manager Ancil, and Mrs. Hoffman, Frank Porcassi, bodyguard; Leo Morrison, Baer's theatrical manager; Dorothy Fields and Jimmy McHugh, the songwriters. These two were writing songs for Max and I was to supply the material for an act and work with Max.

LET'S FACE IT YOU'RE WRONG

I got an offer to replace Danny Kaye in the show "Let's Face It." In New York, when Horace Schmidlapp saw me, he almost flipped. I was very gray and you could see in his face, "This is an old man and the part calls for a young man." My agent explained that I dye my hair. Three weeks of rehearsals and we open in Baltimore. The opening is fine.

All the papers next day liked the show, but the reviewers must have rehearsed. Each one wrote: "While he's a clever guy and we laughed at him, he's no Danny Kaye!" The reviewers in Pittsburgh and Washington must have called each other long distance, because they said the same thing.

Colonel Frank Capra, Major Tony Viellar and Captain David Miller were in Washington at the same time. We had a lot of laughs, but Frank didn't like the "He's no Danny Kaye!" So he sent the Washington critic a telegram which read, "Gary Cooper is no Jack Benny, Fred Allen is no Gracie Allen, Barbara Stanwyk is no Jimmy Stewart. Each one is an individual as is Rubin." Next day the guy had an item in his column that I'm still no Danny Kaye and that I must be nuts, because now I think I'm Frank Capra.

We go to the Selwyn Theatre, Chicago, and for once I get good notices without anyone saying, "He's no Danny Kaye." Of course, no one said I was good either. Then a real pip happens. How good is your memory? Remember the jam I had in the gym aboard the *Berengaria*? Well, I meet the guy again this way:

The manicurist in the Drake Hotel barber shop does not come out even with the barber, so I went to her little table to finish off my shodding. Who came in but the Vulgar Boatman. He looked at me, screwed up the lines around his eyes and started to remove his tie. In the mirror he took another gander at me and you could see that he knew the face but couldn't place it. He started for the chair, changed his mind, walked back to me and asked, "Do I know you from some place?"

I replied with a pretty good Nazi German accent "Cumm clozer, blease," and in a loud whisper, I said into his ear: "I am Heinrich Schluter: I meeted you in ze Shancelry in Berlin; I haff a message for you; I call you at ze offis. Heil!"

He backed off like he was shot, grabbed his coat and left the barber shop. The manicurist said, "You fellows in show business have a load of fun kidding each other, don't you?" I said, yes, and asked her to please hurry, I wanted to get out of there. I had an idea.

Benny Baker was in town with a Shakespearean play. I ran to him and told him what had happened. He thought it was wonderful and for me to carry through my idea, and here is what happened:

I called the man's office (I know the steamship line, but I won't tell you) and said to the girl, "Zis is Heinrich Schluter from Berlin; I vant to schpeak wiss ze Vulgar Boatman." She told me he was not there. I said, "Mizz, find him kivikly." She said he was out of town and I curtly yelled, "Vy do you tell me he is oudt of town ven I jus saw him in ze barber shop of ze Drake Hotel?" She said she was very sorry, but he had been in and hurriedly left the city. I said, "Be sure and tell him vere effer he iss, I find him as I haff a message from ze Feurer." Then I yelled "Heil!" and hung up.

I imagine he took the first train out of town regardless of direction.

LITTLE SIR EGO

When you're called for a Jack Benny show, you never say "I'm going to work," it's like the Lucy Show, or Red Skelton's frolics, no pressure. On most shows a bit player is hardly more than a prop you bounce a gag off.

There were many others, but I'm getting to a point. The point is another comic's head.

This guy is really great, and you'll have to guess his name, because there are about five just like him.

I get a call to do his TV show and leave for rehearsal. Now I've done his show before, the procedure is: Here's your script, you play the so-an-so. Okay, you read it with the cast a couple of times, make changes and go home to learn it.

Next few days, you rehearse some more while he and you, the cast, take direction from the director and producer. Suggestions are given and taken from the camera director, the orchestra conductor and choreographer.

Now that you know the whole technical bit, here's what confronted me when I arrived at the studio this particular time.

There he is at a long table. He is surrounded by a lot of no-talent guys and secretaries. Something new has been added. He now smokes a pipe, smoking it much in the same manner as a country girl smoking her first cigarette to prove she's hip.

Instead of the dance director hiring twelve good dancers as he always does, this boy has ordered fifty to choose from. They were the best looking young kids I'd ever seen and every one an accomplished dancer.

As they danced, he'd look from left to right to those at the table and from grimaces and nods of approval, he chose twelve. I just can't tell you of the frustration of the girls who were dismissed, as they slipped into their frocks and slacks.

I don't know whether you know my racket or not. A seasoned performer can take a dismissal graciously. But these kids must now become liars.

Look, they've had their hair and nails done. They brought their make-up kits. Now they must go home to their little room and cry. And if they have homes with family, are they going to say, "I wasn't picked because I'm a lousy dancer," or "I'm ugly," or "I'm deformed." What can they tell their people or landlady? Worse yet, what do they say to the mirror?

Sure, I know that interviews are part of show business. But you don't take a known definite talent and subject them to amateur night proceedings.

Next there are five well-known actresses who are to read for a small part. As each of them reach the dais composed of the self-styled King of Comics and the Jury of Jehovahs of the Jockstraps, she is subjected to, "Your name, experience, etc.?" She reads, and as she does, the comic does a pan shot with his eyes and the refugees of the Catskills either give him a yes or no.

About that time, the writer of the show saw me sitting about with ten other well-known and solid actors. After exchanging pleasantries and introducing him around, I asked him what they wanted me to play, since they bypassed the usual procedure of giving me a script.

Embarrassed, he said, "You're all up for the same part—a tailor—and you'll have to read for the boy wonder." The reactions from the others was like setting off a chain of firecrackers.

The writer then left saying, "Since he's doing this and intends supervising the music and camera work too, why doesn't he just buy an island and make himself king?"

I had thirty bucks in my pocket and a hundred and something in the bank, but I just couldn't take a chance on blowing my top by belting little Sir Ego and turning over that long table by possibly being told by him that I was inadequate, so I went home.

I'm not against this guy being ambitious. Go ahead, be a director, producer, writer, orchestra leader, choreographer and stick the proverbial broom and sweep the floor, but be a gentleman first.

Don't think that I fear telling you the name of that guy, or anyone else in this thing, I fie on them.

But a publishers' profit on a book can soon become a zero, or even less, if he's nailed by libel suits.

You've just got to hear this.

A minute ago I turned off the TV set after watching the comic and the show I told you about.

The twelve girls he finally picked because of their most beautiful legs, and, in his mind, the best dancers were used as follows:

The scene is a night club and there are many extras in the foreground. The girls enter dancing, I think. I'm not sure because the extras covered them to the extent that you could only see them from the navel up.

They weren't on for more than a minute and a half. This is what he made so many girls unhappy for? Wow!

The part of the sponsor's wife he auditioned five actresses for was given to a middle-aged lady.

Naturally, he picked her over the others for her fine reading and dramatic ability. This is how her years of good theatre were used. He blew flour in her face; he slapped her arms and back, pushed her off a couch onto the floor twice. Got toothpaste in her hair and finally ducked her head into a bowl of water and tore her hair, while giving her a shampoo.

Now comes the part the ten fine actors were to read for his meticulous opinion.

First, you ought to know that all but two of us walked out. Those two suffered through the audition and were turned down. Remember by whom?

So who played the part? One of the best known and finest actors in Hollywood.

Here's the big acting role. He is fitting the comic's partner for a new dinner jacket—pronounced "Tuxeeda" by the catskills of the Catskills. The tailor is going to redo the collar, which is basted —and proceeds to tear it off. The comic enters, and on seeing this, rips the suit off the tailor and makes this profound observation. "Now, see how you like it." Then he pulls the tailor's mustache off and tells him to make himself a new one. Now the tailor, one of the finest talents in show business, gets to do his big acting role. He says, "You don't make mustaches, you grow them." The comic replies, "So, go buy some seeds." And with that he pushes the actor out the door.

Believe me, people, this is not Hollywood. Only the "newees" do this. The psychology is much the same as the nice young private in the army, who all of a sudden was made a sergeant.

Here, take this to get the bad taste out of your mouth.

Louis Edelman, who produces "Make Room For Daddy," invited me to play a barber with the sensational Lebanese, Danny Thomas. He sent a special messenger out to my house in the country with the script.

I studied hard and showed up at the first rehearsal almost letter perfect.

Sheldon Leonard, a great actor who has gone straight, is the director. He, Lou and Danny are there with the rest of the cast. My script is open to page one and I'm ready to show off. The good mornings run into joke telling, and Danny is having a ball, playing with Sherry Jackson and Rusty Hamer, the kids in the show.

Now they must be ready to read. No, a guy brings coffee and starts a half hour of very funny reminiscing. Danny tells of how I was his idol as a kid and did wonderful imitations of me. Lou told of when he was managing the Egyptian Theatre, and he defied the bosses by holding me over one week after the other, until it ran into a year. Shelly tells of how the death of Carole Lombard affected me to the extent I couldn't go on with Jack Benny, and he inherited the "tout" role I'd created.

While I was champing at the bit to read, and they were embarrassing me by showing me so much attention, I loved every minute of it.

Someone says, "Shall we get this turkey on the road?" and Jean Hagen reads the first line. Danny says something, Benny Lesee comes in with the snapper, and they stop. They rehash the lines and make them more logical. As Lou Edelman explained, "If they don't believe the story in the beginning, we lose the audience right now." They go on.

Before I can get to ham it up, they stop a dozen times more. Danny sees the consternation on my face and starts laughing. He addresses the cast with, "Rubin has probably learned his lines, but little does he know, we may change the whole thing." They all laugh.

Shelly Leonard addresses me and with a straight face says, "Listen, actor, I'm the director of this show and hear me good right now. You'll take my directions and act them out to the letter. Now, the first instruction I'm going to give you is, do exactly as we do. If you don't like a line, throw it out. If you've got a funnier line, throw it in. And remember at all times I am a strict boss."

The glow you get working for a bunch of guys like this is better than the money.

I didn't throw anything out and I didn't put anything in. The script was that good. And when a comic with the magnitude of Thomas holds absolutely still and does a perfect straight for a bit player, this is something to behold.

After his "warm up," just before we do the show, he introduces the cast. After what he said about me, Benny, Hope, Gobel and Jerry Lewis should have taken the bow instead of me. Dear God, make room for Danny, he deserves your highest cloud.

While doing Danny's show, ran into Jess Oppenheimer, who created and writes the "I Love Lucy" show. I tell him a new joke, he laughs. I ask him for a job, he stops laughing. A few days later he sent for me and I had a ball with Ball for four days. Doing this show is like working for Jack Benny; no pressure, no lessons in acting given and you laugh more than you work. *And*, they don't pay you off in the dark.

MARQUEE VERSUS TICKERTAPE

Once things got so tough, I looked up to heaven as reverently as I could, I asked. "If, in my whole life You can recall something I did that makes me worthy of help, will You please give it to me now. Since I don't know anything but show business, what else can I do? Is there someone or something I can turn to?"

Stopped the melodramatics long enough to get me some breakfast and went out in the back to do some weeding. There also was the stump of an old tree I wanted out and started by digging around it. The first whack at the ground with the pick, brought me a stinging pain in my left hand. Like a shmo, I had forgotten to take off the ring on my little finger. While removing the ring, an idea hit me. I looked up, thanked God, then sat down on the porch to work out this idea.

The idea was; it is only August and a lot of poeple I know order the Christmas presents they give to family and employees early.

What if I made a connection with a discount jewelry house in Los Angeles to let me open a small but well appointed office in Beverly Hills, with the hundreds of people I know personally, plus some people who knew me, I'd have a hell of a start on the other people I'd seen hustling jewelry to theatrical people. I know, because I've bought from them.

Now! I can't go to these jewelers with my hat in my hand; how can I be sent in, in a way that would sound like I was doing them a favor? I've got it! I know just the guy.

You see, this fellow Bob Fox, who lived here now, worked with some of my brothers for years in the razor blade business.

This has got to be it, because the last I heard Bob was in that type of jewelry business. Got his phone number from my brother, Irving, and called him.

He was cordial and immediately invited me to have lunch with him. I thought I better tell him what was on my mind, because if I was presuming too much, it would give him an out to make that lunch some other time. No, he still invited me after he heard my pitch and I left for his office in Beverly Hills.

After the usual amenities, I impatiently started on my story—his phone rang, he talked for a couple of minutes, wrote out something that looked like an order blank and handed it to a secretary—"As I was saying," I started, but the phone rang again and he went through the same motions as before. When this happened again, he said, "Let's get out of here, and go where you won't be interrupted."

When we sat down in the restaurant, I almost started again with the, "As I was saying" bit, when the waitress came and took our order. Then it hit me, how grateful I was, we were in a hamburger parlor. I wouldn't have had enough money had we gone to the Derby, or one of the costly places he usually goes to.

Bob said, "Look Benny, even with all of the interruptions, I got the gist of what you're thinking of. Now, I know the people you'd like to see and it would be very easy to send you in the right way. Let me make a suggestion first and if you don't like my idea, I'll call some people the minute we get back to my office.

The food came and we talked as we ate. Bob asked, "First of all, do you know what I was doing on the phone, what I was writing and handing to the girl?" I admitted that I didn't. He explained, "From each call I made money. $22.00, $15.00, $32.00, $10.00 and $45.00. Those were orders for stock. I am a customers man for the brokerage house."

I must have said, "You're kidding?" or some such stale remark because he continued as if I had said nothing. "From the way I talk, you know I didn't get past grammar school and my vocabulary is limited; but, having been a salesman and sales manager for years, I do know figures. But you, you know figures, your years of acting has taught you how to talk correctly and most important, your inflections, light and shade and use of dramatics, would make you a hell of a convincing stock salesman."

I should have been flattered, yet what he said left me cold. I'm not as clever with figures as he surmised and having had stock salesmen hustle me, knew I just couldn't sell stocks convincingly. But my answer to him did not belie my thinking. I asked, "How long would it take me to learn the business?" He answered, "I know you're thinking how long will it be before I make a buck. Right?" I nodded yes.

He then laid out this routine. He would ask his boss to put me on, selling me as a smart guy who knew hundreds of celebrities and even tho' I wouldn't be bringing a lot of dough in a hurry, I'd be good publicity for the firm. This he did with great finesse and the boss was glad to have me. Haven't mentioned the firm's name on purpose, because I'll come back to them later.

Bob gave me a lot of material to study after I listened to him work on the phone for about three hours. All the way home I tried to decipher what he was talking about but more important, how sweet it was that every few minutes he made from 10 to 50 dollars.

I read during dinner, after dinner, until midnight. I couldn't digest my dinner, or most of the material. S.A.G.–A.G.V.A.–A.F.T.R.A., I knew, but S.E.C.–N.A.S.D.–N.Y.S.E.–I didn't dig. Debentures preferred dividends, exdividends, arbitrage, long-short-puts and calls befuddled me. Trying to read a balance sheet made me dizzy. I quit and tried to sleep, but no go, so I got up and turned on the T.V. So what was playing? An old movie about a has-been actor who was trying to get back in. He was out because he was a bottle man and nobody would take a chance on him. He was hustling jewelry on movie sets, out of a bag. Nice viewing! For the next two weeks, I studied till eleven, got to Bob's office in time to join him at lunch and suck his brains. Always leaving Bob's phone number with my service in case I might get a call for a job. Listen to him work till three and beat the traffic home on the freeway, then study some more till my eyes wouldn't stay open. I was beginning to dig the stuff pretty good.

Got a call to do the Jack Benny radio show. Rehearse Saturday morning, do the show Sunday. When I got to the studio, Jack said they tried to get me before I left home, to tell me that the "bit" he had for me was out, but I'd get paid anyway since I was called. He did this quite a few times, then I got hip to the fact that there never was that "bit," he was throwing me the dough, without embarrassing me by offering a loan.

After three weeks, Bob thought I was ready to take my tests for a license. There was the Mutual Fund Quiz and the N.A.S.D. test. Arrangements were made and I sat opposite a very serious man. From a sealed envelope, he withdrew a sheaf of papers for himself and a lined sheet for me with about (I don't recall) 100 questions. Oh yes, he handed me an indelible pencil.

When he asked, "Are you ready?" I got a "flop sweat." On the stage this means you've just told your funniest joke and it laid there. You're as cold as ice but you sweat.

Came the questions, one tumbling over the other. I answer bang, bang, bang, with the indelible pencil. Once I stopped and asked, "Can we come back to that?" He answered, "No, now." I hesitatingly wrote what I thought was the answer. My confidence started to give way and started to think, "Suppose those I answered bang, bang, bang, were wrong?" He asked some more I wrote. Then he stopped me cold with this, "Just a minute, has someone briefed you on this test?" I answered, "No, Sir." He said, "You're answering these mathematics too fast, you're not stopping to think." "Are they correct?" I asked. He said, "They are right on the button, you seem to know them by rote."

I said, "So help me God, Sir, I never have heard these before." He said, "Okay, let's take these last figures, show me how you came to the conclusion." "I'm sorry, Sir, but I can't work them out on paper, I do them in my head." I shuttered. He put his pencil down and laughed the coldest laugh I had ever heard. This scared the hell out of me, so I threw in fast, "Look, Mr., if you'll give me some other mathematic problem that is not in the test— and I do it—won't you then believe me?"

He unwrapped the phony laugh, stared at the ceiling for a minute, panned his eyes down to the paper and wrote some figures. Then he broached a problem. I answered it correctly. He looked at me incredulously and in almost a whisper he said, "How?" I told him that I got my arithmetic and percentages from playing horses, shooting craps and paying commission. He said, "This is the first time I ever heard of misspent life paying off legitimately." Yes, I got my license.

Okay, so now I'm in the bag, eh? Just grab a pencil, pick up the phone and like Bob, I'll be counting all that loot that comes in, 10—20—30—50 bucks every few minutes. Nyet!

I'll cut the script way down lest you too get bored and con-fused with details. Two full days to write down every person I could call by their first name. Another day for acquaintances and people I had met or worked with in show business. Came to 2,100 names. Most were rich people.

Composed a letter telling them of my new business. Wrote every address by hand so it wouldn't look like an ad. Signed every letter and wrote something personal on each. Folded, sealed, stamped and mailed them. I dropped them in the post office a few at a time like you'd plant corn, with the prayer that these too would grow and flourish into a new future for me. This was Saturday so that Monday morning I would just sit and wait for the orders to come in.

There were three calls Monday. One wished me luck, another explained that he has had a broker for twenty years and didn't feel like leaving him and the third was beautifully stated. "How the hell I can trust you with my money when you frittered away the fortune you've made?" He hung up before I could correct him on the word fritter.

Came Wednesday and I knew the letters meant nothing. Paid thirty-five bucks for a stock mailing list. Mailed out a thousand, got over nine hundred back—no such person, address unknown and from the balance, nothing. Then I placed an ad in both the Hollywood *Reporter* and the *Daily Variety*. It read: "Today's good stock buys—Phillippine oil at 6 cents per share, or Christiana Securities at 15 thousand dollars a share." The gag brought a great response and I was off to the races. However, it took my brother, Eddie, to break the ice and give me my initial order. The show biz explanation of this would be, "He was breaking in his act on the small time."

The next guy who bought stock didn't pay for it; which meant I had to sell him out at a loss—my loss. Custom decrees that on a non-collectable item, the salesman takes the loss. However, if there is a profit, the reneger gets the profit. "Wha?"

The act progressed nicely as the material got better, meaning—getting away from selling junk.

All of a sudden, I'm getting acting jobs and taking them. The wrinkles are slowly disappearing from the vicinity of the navel.

Then—boing! Fox told me that the rules are a stockbroker cannot have two businesses! I made like I didn't hear nuttin' and continued acting—when I could get it.

Between the stocks and the acting, I've caught the wolf by the tail and slung him into limbo.

Near the end of June, had a misunderstanding with my boss. Quickly it was; a client sold some stock and needed the money right now. The rule reads that she couldn't get it for five days, unless—in some houses—they pay the interest—my client needed every dollar, but my boss wouldn't budge from the five-day ruling.

You know how words on this subject can eventually turn to personalities which have nothing to do with the original argument? Well, they did and I quit. Around about July I got a call from Joe Fields who was with Daniel Reeves. This can become confusing when you speak of someone who is with Daniel Reeves. You could be someone who plays golf with him, you might be a pro-football player who works for him, a hockey player, a pal, or you could be in some charity work of which Dan had more hands in than a centipede; but in this instance, it was in Daniel Reeves stock brokerage firm.

Now this Joe Fields is no relative of the sweet little old Joe of Weber and Fields. This Joe is a nice guy who's home I had been to as a guest. He is a stockbroker with Dan Reeves; but he knows a lot of theatrical people and speaks their jive.

Joe said, "I saw your funny ad in the papers, but didn't take seriously your being in the stock business, until—by accident, of course—you called on one of my clients." "I'm sorry," I started and Joe said, "Sorry for what? Even though he is my client, you were with a different house, so you didn't do anything unethical because we happened to know the same people. But what I didn't understand is, why a headliner played the small time?" My heart jumped a beat. Joe continued, "When can we have lunch and talk? Wait a minute, better than that, I'm eating lunch at home today, Maggie and the kids will be glad to see you, what do you say?" I said, "Yes."

The groceries were good, Maggie graciously sang a song I'd heard her do before. She did this for me and, believe me, for any amount of money I'd never do a show for one person. She did, and beautifully. I repaid them a little with a couple of stories and did my lousy card tricks for the children. Nary a word about business from Joe.

Walking back to his office, I offered myself and he accepted.

Two weeks later, I was sitting opposite Tom Cerny who is one of Dan Reeves' partners. Again I was taking tests. I waltzed through the Mutual Fund and N.A.S.D. tests, but here came a new one and it had me scared to death. The New York Stock Exchange test.

This Tom had two faces. No, he wasn't what two-faced means the way we use the expression. First face first. Stern, business man in the process of rule keeping and staying to the truth. These rules are stringent and you can understand why. The guy—me—was asking for a license to handle millions of dollars of people's money. Any deviations or mis-management would reflect on the firm. Here comes the questions.

The first ten or twelve seem easy, then I answer one and Tom smiles. Not the prop laugh of the first guy—but a genuine smile. Yet, I wasn't sure if the smile was a bit of applause, or what the hell can you expect from an actor, I go on.

We're almost near the end when Tom says, "Don't write the answer to the next one until you've digested it." You see, that pencil is indelible and you can't erase, or retrace words. He asks, I think, but no digesting. The problem sticks in the throat of my mind. Ah, ah, I've got it and I answer verbally. Tom smiles and says, "Let me put the problem to you this way." I try it again mentally, then blurt out the answer. He says, "Write it down." As I do, he continues, "Jokes you can ad lib, but you can't do any gag-switching with a balance sheet." I thank him. We go on.

Only a few questions to go when he asks me a dilly. By the look on my face he knows I'm stymied. He says, "You can't ad lib but I can. Try thinking in terms of paying commission." I do, but since I've paid five and ten percent, these fractions are fracturing me. Then came his other face. He said, "You'll break that pencil the way you've got it gripped." I put it down. Then he told me about seeing me at the Palace in Chicago, remembered part of the bill and a big joke I was telling them. He went thru the whole Gershwin score of "Girl Crazy" that he saw me in at Garrick Theatre. This took about ten minutes.

Don't forget now, this man had other business to attend to—

big business—and here he was losing money and wasting his time to give me a break. All of a sudden, like a flashback, came the answer that he wanted and I gave it to him, loud and clear. He smiled and said—as the Ritz Brothers do—"Don't holler, write!" I wrote, he shook my hand.

"Wait a minute, Mr. Cerny," I said. "What is this rule about no broker can have another business?" He told me that that was correct and it would be a shame to lose these contacts because it could help me in this business. He pardoned himself and went into a huddle with Dan and another partner, Charles Jawitz.

They came to this conclusion. A letter to the New York Stock Exchange, explaining my unique situation. Quick answer was, I would be allowed five days a month in theatricals. That is if I passed the tests and character references.

Now all I had to do is wait and see if N.Y.S.E. okays my application for the license. And in the meantime I'll try and get some acting jobs—wait a minute—hold the phone, I forgot something that might kill me with the N.Y.S.E. I interrupted Mr. Cerny to tell him I neglected to mention about having been in reform school. He just stared at me a minute, then asked his secretary, Eleanor McDaniel, to bring him my application.

I told him the true circumstances and the dates. He dictated the facts and the girl typed them in at the bottom of the application. All he said to me was, Rotts of Ruck. Up to now, Miss McDaniel was very pleasant to me. Now, she was laughing. She could see by my face that I was puzzled by her gaiety then said, "Big bad man eleven years old; I bet you used a water pistol."

Came two small parts at M.G.M. and a couple of Jack Benny's.

Almost three weeks to the day, the application came back from the N.Y.S.E. There was a notation at the bottom. "We knew all about Mr. Rubin's sojourn at the 'Industrial School for Boys' at Shirley, Massachusetts, and that did not constitute a felony." They gave me my license.

For almost seven years I had the pleasure of doing both, until Irving Fein who handles Jack Benny's publicity asked me to help out a young fellow who was doing a profile on Jack's life. I had helped other writers do this for the New York *Post*. This has nothing to do with the story, but I've got to throw it in. Jack saw me sitting with the man and said to me, "Stop making me such a nice guy, tell him about some of my faults." During our talk it came out about my wearing two hats.

Evidentally, this man couldn't figure, or didn't believe that the one man out of thousands of stockbrokers had this special dispensation from the New York Stock Exchange, had to be an actor.

He checked to verify the story and was told that it was true, but I had gotten too much publicity and as of that day they recinded my special permission.

My bosses told me that I'd have to make up my mind right then, if I was going to be a broker or an actor. I resigned.

A STAH IS BAWN

I put together what I thought was a different kind of an idea for the Palace in New York, called Al Melnick, my agent. I explained the idea and when I arrived, he had already sold the idea to Jack Haley.

Jack had faith in my material, but fortified his own single act by going to Eugene Conrad for comedy material. Then we took every bit of material, brushed up some of the stuff and wrote a lot of new things. We lined up some people and broke the material in at the Eighty-Sixth Street Theatre. After sifting the wheat from the chaff we opened at the Palace. We were a smash hit. I'll not go into any ham about ourselves or the jokes, but one bit we did I'd like to talk about.

During Cantor's and Jessel's long run at the Palace, they sang a song called "Pals," written for them by Abel Baer. They sang a verse and chorus and while the orchestra played a beautiful dramatic melody as background music, they reminisced about their childhood and days with Gus Edwards. It was as lovely a story as you could listen to. People cried and cheered at the finish.

Soooo, I paraphrased the song. (It took me a long time to convince Jack to do it, because he was afraid of repercussions from Cantor and Jessel fans.) Our lyrics explained that we were *not* with Gus Edwards because he wouldn't have us. Then we reminisced as the original kids did it, only we were from Boston and ate at each others' houses. The wrong days for the wrong foods.

At the finish we proved our friendship by giving each other the shirts off our backs, climaxed it by swapping pants. It played a lot funnier than it reads.

Haley had a picture commitment after our run in the Palace, so he went to Hollywood while I booked a few weeks with Fanchon and Marco, winding up in San Francisco at the Warfield Theatre. The house orchestra had a new college kid at the head of it. His name was Horace Heidt.

While there I got a contract for a radio show with the Shell Oil Company. The sponsor liked Heidt, too, and we worked together.

Del Crespi, an ex-ball player, had an idea to take a big Oakland dance hall and roller skating rink, and convert it into a night spot. Would I allow him to put my name up in lights? Would I let him! Was he crazy? Of course I would—especially, since he gave me half of the joint without putting up a quarter. My name in lights must have been seventy-five feet in length.

The place seated eight hundred people, at a buck a pop. During the opening night there were over eleven hundred such admissions. They didn't spend much, though, because booze was against the law at the time. Sam Fischer, my personal manager, caught employees stealing the first night. This continued, but the pay-off pilfering was when he took a layer of garbage from a can and found three or four sheets of wax paper covering steaks, chops and chickens.

I still had the radio show for plenty of money, so the financial part of the venture didn't bother me. Also I commuted from Hollywood so I was near my family.

Corresponding with Haley all this time, I found that in a few weeks we'd both be free. We agreed to return as partners. We booked the Palace again, with a week at the Albee Theatre in Brooklyn to break in some new material. We were going to be different from all other acts.

Jack came to New York, we rehearsed and opened at the Albee in Brooklyn. It was fine.

Melnick came to see us. The show we were to follow was such a big hit, Arthur Willi wanted to hold it for two more weeks. We agreed and he gave us both surprises. He booked Jack to make a film and I was to make a short comedy for Warner Brothers in their studio on Long Island.

Two weeks later, we were making the last shot in the picture and I was exhausted, working eight and nine hours a day. Well, tomorrow looked good; the Palace, only two shows a day and happiness with Haley. Willi had allowed us to pick our acts and we were set with bits for Bea Lillie, George Olson and some others.

My last picture shot was in a bed. Good, I'd relax and work at the same time. When the scene was over, the director said, "Cut, we've got it in the can." I did not hear him, as I was out cold. They brought me to and I went home in a cab, sick as a dog. My wife took one look at me, called Melnick and he called Doctor Amy. The three of us went to his office and he gave me a thorough examination. If I didn't have my appendix out immediately it might burst.

I turned out to be a coward. Wasn't there another way besides the knife? I'd heard they could be frozen. On and on I went, walking in and out of offices, in and out of the men's room. Finally, mad at everybody, I decided, "If we can do it now, okay, otherwise I won't do it!"

Dr. Amy advised a night's sleep first, and then preparation for the operation. "No!" I yelled, "Now or nothing! No preparation, no nothing, now!" The kindly doctor said, "Okay, son, let's go." I could have died, but there was no way out.

In front of the hospital I considered running—but my ego stopped me. There stood an intern with a wheel chair. He asked, "Is this the patient?" I yelled, "I don't need that, I can walk!"

Up the elevator, down a hall, into a room. The smell of ether got me; I was going into my yelling routine when Doctor Amy quietly said, "Yes, my boy, no enemas, no nothing. Now!" Undressed, went for the shave and insisted on walking to the operating room.

Then I went into the following without hardly taking a breath. I did three of my best jokes—no laughs—I read the last line of a very big joke like this, "I thought he wanted to make blintzes, so I gave him an egg the Lord is My Shepherd I shall not want" Yisskadahl vey iss kadahsh shmay raboh (prayer for the dead) up to this point, Mary has dabbed her eyes with a kerchief—now she was stuffing it in her mouth to keep from laughing.

When I saw all those baby spotlights over my head and the anesthetist lowering a cone over my nose, I said, "Mary, if anything happens to me," the answer to this and the last words I heard came from the understanding heart and beautiful mind of Doctor Amy;

those memorable words were, "Oh shut up!"

Al took the news to Willi, who asked Haley to go in with someone else. Jack wouldn't think of it. Willi was in a tough spot, as Holtz, Cantor, Jessel, Benny, Fay, Baker and Richman were not available.

(In desperation Arthur called Jake Lubin, head of the Marcus-Loew booking office. Mr. Lubin told Arthur that the only free comic around was going into Loew's State the following week. After some pleading, Mr. Lubin released Milton Berle and he went into the big time, never to leave it.)

HAMTRAMCK

I played the Bowery Cafe in 1942. The place was run by Frank Barbaro, a marvelous character. He was the owner, producer, director, and got top billing over everybody else. There was a banner out in front with his picture on it, which also adorned every mirror in the joint.

Guests paid an admission before entering, so he could afford Sophie Tucker, Tony Martin, and other famous names. You sat at a table twenty by twenty inches square; there were five hundred of them, seating around two thousand paying guests. There was no room on the tables for food and Frank didn't want you to eat, anyway. The head waiters were all professional wrestlers and, if someone got out of order, one of them would pick up a party of four and carry them out bodily. No rough stuff, though; nobody got hurt; it was all done nice and easy in a gentlemanly sort of way. The shows started at nine o'clock and went on without a let-up until one-thirty in the morning. It was always continuous, terrific entertainment. The waitresses were expert at grabbing your glasses just before they were empty. And Frank never gave you a chance to get up and dance, or even consider going home.

Frank loved actors so much that he bought the adjacent property for a fat figure and built dressing and play rooms for the performers. There was a private shower attached to each dressing room. Frank wouldn't let any of the actors working for him spend a dime; it was all on the house and welcome. Frank had a strange fetish: he liked to be mistaken for Leo Carrillo. And we actors always made it a point to do so.

I arrived around seven that first night, hung up a few suits in my dressing room, and waited to go on. Arthur Treacher was in town with "Panama Hattie" and he brought out a gang for my opening. I saw him through the peephole and went over to his table for a quick hello. Barbaro saw me and gave me a funny look that had me wondering but I shrugged it off as just opening night nerves.

I got on stage at about one-ten and came off at one-forty. My act didn't take a half-hour but now we were in World War II and I sold bonds to the customers. I remember that the biggest buyer among the ladies talked direct to Ray Milland on long distance, and the top buyer of the men spoke to Ginger Rogers. The band took five and the ladies of the ensemble were on again. Then I came back for a few minutes until the two o'clock curfew, and the show was over.

I caught Treacher before he left, thanked him and said good night. Then someone told me that Barbaro wanted to see me in his office. I hunted him up and listened as he gave out in his heavy Italian accent. He had a funny habit of using adages without knowing their endings but I kept as solemn as a brick wall.

"Looka, keed," Frank said, "you awright. But please no go in oriense (audience) befo' the show. People comin' here for see you. Ef you go roun' a tables, they see you, so they go home. Rememb' familiyarity is a whata you callem."

"Yes, Sir," I replied in my most formal manner.

"Nuther t'ing, Benny, lax a lax, you too steef. You stand one place, no wrinkle a sleefs. Move round, lax a lax."

"Yes, Sir."

"I bawl you out," Frank continued. "Now I make you happy. I gonna keep you nuther couple weeks. You happy, no?

I explained to this princely fellow that I appreciated his kindness but contracts were already signed for the next two weeks in Covington.

He shrugged his shoulders in a gesture of helplessness. "I do my besta to give," he said, "but he not take." Then he added some well-meant advice. "I'm glad you work; but jumpin' roun', jumpin' roun' one place to nother ats no good. Ain't you know a rolling stone is a whata you callem?"

When my week at the Bowery ended, generous-hearted Frank Barbaro threw a big party for me with all the trimmings. Goodbye and good luck to you, Leo Carrillo.

TABLE FOR TWO

Comes a time in every actor's life, when he's between jobs.
I was in the middle of a long intermission when, one morning Sid
Rogell phoned me. I thought he wanted to set up a heart game
but Sid mentioned a man named Guissardi, who owned the commissary at R.K.O. It seemed that he had just split up his partner-
ship with John Steinberg, now manager of the Hillcrest Country
Club in Los Angeles. They had jointly owned the Victor Hugo
Restaurant in Beverly Hills. Steinberg had been welcoming guy
because of his New York experience. Neither Guissardi nor his
sons knew the celebrities who visited the Victor Hugo and, now
that Steinberg was out, they were on a spot to keep the patronage
coming.

Sid had told Guissardi that his worries were over if he could
get a certain fellow to front the place. This man, Sid said, was a
very wealthy actor who was tired of the game and had just refused
three thousand a week for a nation-wide tour. However, he was
crazy about the cafe business, knew show business upside down,
and was well liked by all the stars, whom he knew intimately.

Guissardi, as Sid told it to me, leaped at the prospect of getting such a fabulous fellow to keep the Victor Hugo popular with
the movie colony. Sid told the restaurateur that this star would
be hard to get but maybe it could be arranged if he was offered a
percentage of the profits and, meanwhile, was given, oh, say, a
mere hundred and fifty a week to help pay gas and oil for his car.

"Well," I said impatiently, after listening to this long spiel
over the phone, "why bother me? I got my own troubles."

"Don't be so uppity," Sid came back at me. "This dream

character I was promoting to Guissardi is you!"

I immediately started to drop dead; but I changed my mind and got up again, still holding the phone in a rigor mortis grip. Even if Gabriel had blown his trumpet, I wouldn't have let go. Eventually I located my voice somewhere down in my shoes and it came to life again.

"I double accept," I said hoarsely. "My big thanks for a big deal," I said. "Howis about hearts tonight?" and we played, him, me, Pete Smith and Parkyakarkas.

Among the generous pack of lies Sid told the man was one fact—I did know the picture stars. Yet not enough of them came into the Victor Hugo to show a solid profit. I kicked the mental gong around and finally came up with an idea that would either make or break the joint . . . or me. It wasn't such a long chance at that as I engaged a name band that was sure to pack them in— Benny Goodman's.

But as per usual, I almost muffed it. When Benny opened, the news hadn't got around as yet and we had only a few tables filled at dinner time. Benny's playing was sensational, of course. But at that hour, especially with an empty room, I felt that the brass, saxes and drums were working too hard. They played so loud that you couldn't hear yourself think.

I waved to Benny, saying with my hands that less fortissimo would be better; but he ignored me. When I tried again I could see him going into a slow burn. And when the band took five, he came over and blasted me out louder than he had played. He laid down the law in no uncertain terms: a "head waiter" wasn't going to tell him how to play.

Naturally I didn't like taking it, but fortunately I didn't blow my cool. I needed the job so I swallowed my pride. However, I was determined not to take anybody's guff laying down and the next day I went into training on the ranch. I swore that on closing night I'd wrap his clarinet around Benny Goodman's neck.

But by Saturday night the till was overflowing with lovely money and all I saw of the Guissardis was their shining teeth as they cracked wide smiles. That was the end of my mad at Goodman. I loved him for having made me look good and would have told him so; but he was still uppity and ignored me.

No, you can't miss with Goodman; but he was off on Sundays so I had a new problem. The youngsters would stop by in the late afternoon for dancing, and then the celebs would come in for dinner and entertainment. A disappointed Sunday night crowd would kill us but what to do? I worked fast and got Jerry Lester, a really funny guy, and filled in with a couple more acts. Now I had to have the basic—the band. I called up all the agents I knew and finally one of them sent over a kid named Kenny Baker, no relation to the tenor.

Comes Sunday night the dinner crowd is stupendous. We seat seven hundred fifty and we've got standees. My head waiter stood behind the ropes refusing lush tips for tables.

Back in the kitchen I had planted some items that weren't on the menu. Chicken noodle soup with motzoh balls for George Levee; potato pancakes for George Burns; Kalok water for Gus Kahn; chopped liver for Pete Smith. I made sure that no salt was put on the food for the diabetics.

Everything went well and the show was socko. Kenny Baker played softly during dinner without being asked, he accompanied the acts to perfection, and then made the joint jump to his rhythm. Benny Goodman came in when the place was really rocking, scowled for a second or two, but finished up dancing on the floor hot as a smoking pistol. Mickey Rooney and Sidney Miller brought along a gang that took over and put on a show better than our own. It was a highly successful evening and I was happy to have had a part in it, even though I was on the sidelines.

I kept up the bluff that I was a rich actor who had condescended to front for a restaurant mostly for the fun of it, and after a few weeks I braced Mr. Guissardi and gently reminded him of the percentage I had been promised. He immediately got his sons together and they offered me twenty-five percent of the profits. I wanted to grab it but I pretended to hedge and suggested ten percent of the gross instead. They okayed the deal and made a date to meet with their attorney, who was out of town, a week from the following Monday.

Milton Sperling was going to marry the youngest of Harry Warner's daughters—Sigmund Romberg had asked me to fix up a nice table for his guests at dinner the night of the wedding. The kids were to be married right after the dinner hour.

On the table I had a little toy camera for the Eddie Black-burns (he's Eastman Kodak in Hollywood), miniature pianos for Jerry Kern and Romberg, dice and roulette for the Bischoffs, a ball and glove for Harry Ruby, and fifty-two Queens of Spades for Sid Rogell, the heart player who had gotten me this job. The table was in the best spot in the room and there were flowers for the ladies, of course.

The first to show up were the Bischoffs. Sam said he was glad to see me and Hatti murmured something. Just a little later Sam beckoned me to the bar. He said that over a thousand people would attend a dinner and show at Earl Carroll's Theatre-Restaurant Sunday night and it might be a good idea for me to go on. I said that I'd be happy to but first I'd have to get permission from my boss to have the evening off.

Later I told Mr. Guissardi about the benefit and he thought it would be good business for me to appear. On Sunday afternoon I went over to Carroll's and rehearsed with the orchestra. It was Manny Klein's music. Murray Cutter had arranged the score for me to fit Bob Mitchum's "Refugee." This, Bob Mitchum wrote for me when he was a budding song writer, with no thought of becoming an actor. That evening Al Rogell, Sid's uncle, greeted me backstage. I explained that I hadn't worked for a long time and was going to take a walk and rehearse. While I was walking, Guissardi came in and Al sat him with Sid, Marge and Pete Smith, Harry Joe Brown and Sally Eilers.

The show moved along beautifully. Al Rogell apologized for having me follow Slapsie Maxie Rosenbloom. I told him that I didn't mind since I wasn't going to do a comic routine. That opened his eyes but I didn't offer any further explanation. Maxie was a smash hit with his act. Then I heard myself introduced and walked on to a good hand.

The leader brought down his baton and the orchestra went into a symphonic arrangement of *America*, the accompaniment for my recitation for the dramatic oratory "The Refugee" Bob Mitchum had written for me.

This was my biggest success. With the finish, cheering shrilled over the heavy applause and I took many bows. When the house was quiet again, I heard that Pete Smith told everyone around him that they ought to be ashamed of themselves for not giving me any work in my profession. "The poor bastard is broke," he angrily concluded, "and because of you he has to work as a greaseball in a restaurant!"

Back on my job that night at the Victor Hugo, I was table-for-twoing when in walked a guy with a kisser full of whiskers. His face was familiar to me—Orson Welles. With him was a curly-haired boy by the name of Joe Cotton, Everett Sloane—Ray Collins and several other Mercury players. As I moved around I could feel Orson's eyes fixed on the back of my head.

Mr. Guissardi returned from the charity affair at Earl Carroll's, said he had seen me on stage, and complimented me on being a fine actor. I thanked him and took the opportunity to ask what time next day we were going to see his lawyer about my percentage.

"I'm canceling the date with the lawyer," he said.

"But why, Mr. Guissardi? You and your sons promised me ten percent of the gross."

"Ten percent of nothing you'll get," he said with finality. "You're a phony!"

"But I know everybody and," I reminded him, "I got them to come here. Look around you; the place is packed."

"Makes no difference," he growled. "Tonight I heard Pete Smith say that you were broke and couldn't get a job in show business. You came here under false pretenses."

And there I was all mixed up again. Background said, "Walk out," temper said, "Belt him one," heart said, "Cry." Though I had the chills I was dizzy with the heat. Anything could have happened. But just then George, one of the captains, called my name and said that Orson Welles wanted to see me.

When I got to his table, Orson said that he and his friends had come in to see me perform on the floor. So I had to explain that I wasn't at the Victor Hugo in my professional capacity but as the manager of the restaurant. When Orson put it to me straight, I had to admit that I would much rather be acting. Then he told me about his radio show, Campbell Soup Playhouse, offered me a part, and I accepted with alacrity.

That was how an unpredictable fate made an important decision for me, with the unconscious help of Mr. Guissardi. When the place closed for the night, Orson was still there and suggested that we adjourn down the street to Armstrong Schroeder's restaurant for a little privacy.

"You seemed to recognize me tonight," the whiskered genius said when we were seated. "You came right over to my table."

"It was your voice," I said. "For you that beard is no disguise."

"What," he asked, "have you heard about me as a person?"

"If you want it straight, I've heard that you are a self-styled genius, a fresh guy, and a fag."

I wouldn't have blamed him if he had hit me. Instead, he let out a booming laugh, and then spoke to me soberly.

"Put yourself in my place. You're on WPA for around eighty bucks a month. Someone tells you that you're a genius. Should you deny it? Or should you admit the infamous charge and accept a hundred thousand for a movie and another bundle for a radio program?"

"I would accept the title of genius," I honestly answered, and I'd do all I could to live up to the part."

"Then we agree," he said with a friendly smile.

Then he told me that he was going to direct his first picture, *Citizen Kane*. And he admitted that while he had directed many plays, when it came to movies he didn't even know where to set up a camera to get what he wanted. So I tried to be a wise guy and, yanking an old envelope out of my coat pocket, started to show him how to lay out establishing shots, medium shots, two shots, closeup and protective close shots. And while I was doing the talking, this terrific genius acted very humble and just kept on yessing me.

Winding up my act as an advisory committee of one, I told him that most directors give a party after a picture is completed but that he should have his before he started shooting. Invite the publicity boys and every technician, even to the prop men and grips, out to his house for a real shindig. Let them see that he's a regular guy. I also suggested that he get a camera man by the name of Greg Toland. "Don't tell him anything," I warned. "Just ask questions." And I advised him to have his rushes, the daily work, sent to his home and not under any circumstances let the bosses see a single foot of film until he himself was satisfied that it was right.

Orson went for everything I told him and when we broke up early the next morning, he shook my hand and grinned his okay.

Now I was positive that I'd go on Orson Welles' radio show and become a member of the Mercury players. I sang all the way as I drove home through the canyons to my chattel mortgage in the valley.

During the week I played hearts with my gang, Smith, Rogell and Parky, went to football games with Gus Kahn. There was no call from Guissardi and no word from Welles.

Then bang! the phone rang. It was Mr. Orson Welles and he gave me the hour for rehearsal.

All night I banged my head against the pillow. What if I can't compete with those New York actors? They're schooled in dramatics; they've proved themselves. I had heard them many times and they were wonderful. But wait, why am I beating myself? I came up the hard way in the theatre. No dramatic classes, no direction, no nothing. I am a long-time graduate *cum laude* of the glaring spotlight. Why, I have stood under it longer than these kids have lived.

Rehearsal was at eight in the morning. We don't go on till five in the afternoon, with a rebroadcast at six. I was blinking and nervous from lack of sleep. Welles nodded to me as I came in. I met his partner John Hauseman, Joe Cotton, Ray Collins, Everett Sloan, Agnes Moorehead, and Vachtangoff. Most of them were wearing chin muffs like Orson's. I found out that they were a hangover from some play they had done in New York; and they were needed again for Welles' first picture. William Powell and Paulette Goddard came in and we all sat around a big table.

The scripts were handed out and we were told what parts we were to read. Welles warned us that he might switch people and parts after the first reading. I was to read Slimane, the detective, and an Arab stool pigeon by the name of Arbi.

Suddenly Orson realized that the sterling actor, Ray Collins, had no part. He became Slimane. The cast started the reading and I got panicky. My stomach began to dance but they didn't need a belly dancer in the show. Closer and closer they came to my lines and still I didn't have the faintest idea what an Arab should sound like. I had heard Ghandi on the radio once and I tried to recall his accent. I got so frightened that I almost jumped up and walked out of there. Jolson did it before a big New York opening. Not having Jolie's kind of money, I stayed.

The actors kept on reading. My eyes stared at the two lines that Arbi had to speak. Then I heard my cue. I said what was written on the paper and I was through with that scene. Orson ignored me and the cast didn't look up as I spoke my lines. Hey, maybe I'm pretty good at that! But I couldn't kid myself about that Arab lingo. It was Amos and Andy's Brother Crawford with a British accent.

There were more lines for me—I got through them somehow—and finally the reading was over. Orson threw his script up in the air.

"Ladies and gentlemen," he said in his cultured tones, "I do not know what this story is about. I saw it on the screen and I have read it carefully but I know it not. What I heard just now was the gawd-damnedest conglomeration of accents and dialects I have ever heard in my life!"

If he means me, I thought, I'll slap him right in that beaver with the script. But Mr. Welles crossed me up again. He tangled with a few of the others but left me strictly alone. Maybe he never heard of Amos and Andy and didn't recognize my swipe. He gave me another small part to play; and there were two more readings at the table. Now we were ready to get on our feet before the mikes. But before we started, Welles had coffee and "shneken" brought in for everybody. Then to work.

Orson stood on a small podium, earphones adorning his skull. A music rack held his script, and beside him were a row of buttons: one for the music, some for signals to mikes in other rooms. Welles, you see, is a realist: when in the script you are supposed to go into another room, you don't just suppose, you go into another room.

We all whacked our brains out for eight solid hours, until four o'clock in the afternoon. Then the script was cut for size: one hour for the first show, fifty-five minutes for the second, when Elmer Davis did a five-minute news spot. The legit actors all turned out to be regular people and we coffeed together until it was time to go on the air.

Now came that moment when you either did or you didn't. No retakes like in the movies. Welles had a big cigar in his mouth.

He pushed a button and Bernie Herman started the orchestra on "Tonight We Love." With the wave of one hand, Orson faded the music down and, with the other, he beckoned the announcer to make with the words. The man introduced Orson, who removed the cigar and began to speak. His beautiful voice is hypnotic and winds itself around your heart. Then his wiggling fingers started the sound effects and the play was on.

Down near the finish I had a scene with Welles as Pepe Le Moko. He was supposed to choke me, as Arbi, for squealing on him. Naturally, he doesn't actually choke me; I've got to get it over with my voice. It isn't an easy effect to do. But just before the scene, Orson came over and handed me a small glass of sour pineapple juice. Then I was able to choke and make it sound genuine.

After the final curtain came down, the credits were read. Everybody but me was mentioned as the announcer went through the list. Then when it sounded as though he was through, he gave me a puff, throwing in phrases like "that inimitable actor" that Spencer Tracy would have been proud of. The other members of the cast looked my way and beamed their approval. What kind hearts and gentle people!

As soon as the sign-off signal was flashed, I went over to Welles to thank him. But before I could open my mouth he ordered everybody to sit down to go through the five-minute cut in the script. When that was in shape, it was time for the second broadcast.

Now that the day's work was finally done, I approached Welles again to offer him my thanks. But he gave me a brief, "Don't go away," and went around shaking hands with people and talking. When we were at last alone, he never mentioned the show, the performance, or even acknowledged my sincere thank you.

"Let's have dinner," he abruptly suggested.

I wasn't shaved and we were both without ties, but it didn't matter as we ate at his home, just the two of us. After dinner, when we were relaxed, I thanked him again for the nice plug on the air. He waved it away with his hand and told me that while I had done a good job, the plug was particularly meant for the producers and directors of other radio shows. Since they all listened to his program, the plug should result in some jobs for me.

Orson Welles didn't have to go out of his way for me. We were not in the same class, socially or intellectually, and he owed me no favors. What he did came out of the bigness of the man. I was a respected "Mercury" player for two years and when it ended I did get a lot of important radio jobs.

THE BIRTH OF TELEVISION

If I start you out with, "In nineteen thirty, George Jessel, Harry Hershfield, Bugs Baer and I were on our way to New Jersey to do a show," if you're fortyish—or over—, your first guess would be that we were going someplace to play a benefit.

If you're thirtyish—or younger—, your first guess would be a question; "Who the hell *were* you?"

You oldies cool it, while I clue in the "Newies" as to who we were. Arthur (Bugs) Baer was probably the most quoted and copied columnist of his day.

Harry Hershfield the most popular cartoonist, and a raconteur second to none.

George Jessel at thirty two had been a headliner for nearly twenty years.

I was the baby at thirty one; with experience in every phase of show business since nineteen fourteen.

A scientist and engineer by the name of Alan B. Dumont had invited us to appear on a new type of entertainment he called Television. WHO DAT?

When we arrived at his studio, we saw banks of lights and a big box. Mr. Dumont laid this on us. We would perform in front of the big box; it would take our pictures, send them thru a wall, up in the air over the Hudson River, thru the walls of the Ambassador and Waldorf Astoria hotels, into a box in the suites occupied by General Sarnoff and William S. Paley. I think you would have said what we said, "This guy is bananas."

The four of us were expert at putting on stage make-ups (all performers were). Take a tube of "Steins" grease paint and make dots. With four fingers blend them in all over your kisser and neck. With middle finger a dot of rouge, blend that in, and with the pinkie, make cupid bows on the lips. Dip the powder puff into a box of powder and pat your face with it until there was no trace of grease. A small soft brush removed the excess powder, then with the tip of the tongue you licked the powder from your lips. Deftly with a moistened forefinger remove the powder from the eye lashes and gently brush the upper up and lower down. No matter what you looked like to others, to you, you were a doll!

All of our expertise went out the window when a Mickey Angelo painted our faces green and our lips brown. . . . Do you know why? Me neither.

With no audience the show goes on. First a gal by the name of Seaby sang beautifully. Ain't that a gas! I can remember Seaby but can't recall her first name. It's ten to one it was Mary.

Bugs did a funny monologue on current events. Jessel did his "Mama on the telephone" routine and some jokes with Hungarian flavor. Hershfield told jokes with a Hebrew accent. I told myself, "Boychik you daid." Those accents were my stock in trade; so even before Flip Wilson was born, "the Devil made me do it." I told nothing but Irish jokes with a heavy brogue.

As a true vaudevillian and a bonafide ham, my next line should be "I killed the people. I laid them in the aisles." Tho there wasn't any people I knew I was a hell of a hit—and I'll sign an affidavit—I saw one of those big New Jersey mosquitoes on the wall laughing his head off.

PRESENT SHOCK

Webster's definition of "frustration" is easy to read and very easy to digest, but have you ever eaten it?

The year was 1972. It was about five o'clock in the evening. I was having a quarrel with my memory box about certain dates. The reason for trying for total recall was I was putting together seventy-three years of memories for a book to be titled: *Come Backstage With Me.*

My fingers were hurting from the ridges on the pencils and my belly was asking, when? already.

While swining it up in the kitchen, I noticed in TV Guide that they were going to telecast the premier of a picture. This I wanted to see because from 1927 to 1930 I broadcast every premier and interviewed the stars in the forecourts of Grauman's Chinese, the Egyptian and in the lobbies of Carthay Circle, Pantages and Mayan Theatres.

I wanted to see how the new breed handled the stars. Naturally, I was going to compare and give myself the best of it. I don't know of anybody who likes me better than me.

After the navel stretching, I selected the channel, made myself comfortable in the corner of the couch and watched the news telecast. I don't think I got past Spiro Agnew hitting someone with a golf ball before I fell asleep.

Hey, wait a minute! What are Pete Smith and Howard Strickling doing in my brain? Each of them had a phone and were belting at me. I answered their hollering with: "Yes, I'll be there an hour early to entertain the fans in the bleacher seats. Don't I always? . . . What? . . . Don't deviate from the typed cards you give me for the introduction of the stars? . . . Yeh, yeh, good taste! . . . What? . . . Not make fun of the celebs who say 'I'm glad to be here and I know I'll enjoy the picture?' Okay, okay. . . . No, Pete, no cracks like I made at the *Red Dust* opening about Harlow must have mislaid her underwear, or at the *Gay Divorcee* about Chaplin speaks American with an English accent, but thinks like a Russian . . . . Yes, Howard, I know she looks lovely, didn't I just spend a month at San Simeon? . . . What? Look, Pete, that guy who came with Sid Grauman looked exactly like the colored bass singer at the Orpheum. How could I possibly know he was the Maharajah of Indore, or outdoor, or wherever the guy shoots tigers? . . . Yes, yes, yes, I'll use good taste . . . . Okay, goodbye."

Then, somewhere in my disturbed sleep, I saw a big box with letters on it. A man was using it like you would a camera. Why ain't I there? Some guy was talking for me. My God, I missed the opening! What'll Mr. Meyer say? Hold it! The guy who was taking my place is introducing LIBBER what? Who's that Raquel gal, half-dressed? And Jane somebody who was making a fist at the camera. And who the hell are Rock, Tab, Rip, Chuck, Sonny, Cher, and what the hell is a three dog night—or an Engelbert Humperdinck?

Wait a minute! What does that TEL-A-VISION mean? What is it? There's Frank Capra, Barbara Stanwyck, Norma Shearer, Mary Pickford and Buddy Rogers, but the interviewer doesn't know who they are.

The phone rang. That must be Pete, or Howard to tell me I'm late and—it isn't either one of them, it's someone who dialed incorrectly.

My eyes were open and I was staring at the TV set. In my ears were voices yelling, "You're late, you're late." Yes, the big floodlights were on, there were cameras everywhere and the people were wearing kahkamaimee clothes. Not one of them said, "I'm glad to be here and I know I'll enjoy the picture."

One man in a tuxedo-like sweater expressed all of the glamour with, "Ain't this a gas!" Another young guy with long hair had his bowtie tucked under his collar and he expressed his opinion of the new picture by saying, "I heard that this gig is a grabber!" Then all eyes turned to the left as someone said, "Here's the

King!" I strained my eyes to see Gable, but no; into view came a young lad with a stone face like a statue, long sideburns and five bodyguards, who all wore small guitars in their lapels.

Boy, was I late!!! Forty-four years late!

INTERVIEW WITH BENNY RUBIN
by
John E. DiMeglio
Mankato State College, Minn.

A man who has been a key figure in American popular culture since he got his first professional job in show business in 1914 is Benny Rubin. His career has included tabloid shows, showboats, burlesque, vaudeville, night clubs, Broadway shows, radio, movies, and television. That career has encompassed the worst and the best aspects of the world of entertainment, from living in the "flea bag" hotels to starring as a headliner at the one and only Palace. The veteran performer lives today in a Hollywood apartment which features walls covered with framed glossies that trace much of his career and commemorate many of his colleagues, past and present.

Approaching the age of seventy-three Rubin remains active in his profession, writing and starring in a "Gunsmoke" episode, appearing as a character actor on several other television programs, and guest-shotting on various discussion shows. Identified very often as a regular on the past Jack Benny shows, Rubin's most recent artistic accomplishment was headlining in a special television tribute to vaudeville, an NBC presentation hosted by Johnny Carson.

What follows is the result of several hours of a tape-recorded interview which the author enjoyed with Rubin in the summer of 1969 and has been edited by the author.[1]

JD. Benny, how did you begin your show business career?
BR. My first professional job was in what was called a tab show. The tab show is what the name implies. It's a tabloid of a musical show. There were ten people with this show and the man who owned the show would steal a Broadway show and do it in tabloid form. It was really more or less a long vaude-

ville act. My first salary was $16 a week, set at that figure because I was getting $15 a week as a rubber heel salesman and when I went from amateur nights into professional, I demanded one dollar more than I was getting as a salesman. In those years, $16 meant that you would have room and board for six bucks a week, that you could send your mother five bucks a week, and have a lot of money left to blow. Sixteen bucks—it was great. My next job was on a showboat and that was great, too. I got the same money, sixteen bucks, but we called it sixteen and cakes. Cakes meant that the performers got their food free of charge. On a showboat, we had ten in a show, six girls and four men. Now, those girls were twelve and thirteen years old and had their mothers with them. Their mothers did the cooking and the laundry and, even though there was no reason—I was fourteen years old, so what?—they also protected their daughters. Naturally, on a showboat, we also got our room free, so we had what we called cabins and cakes. From showboats I went to burlesque. In burlesque, I began to meet hotel rooms, which I never had before. In the old boardinghouses and the first hotels that I stayed at, there was no such thing as room and bath. The bathroom was down the hall and I'll never forget this line as long as I live because I always heard it—when you'd knock on the door, some guy would yell, 'Be out in a minute!' At that point in my career, those hotels cost a buck and a half a day. Well, when I signed on with burlesque, I got sixty bucks a week and I quickly graduated to the point where I paid two dollars a day, which meant one thing. It marked the first time I had a sandbox right in my room. Oh, boy, that was a pleasure. I didn't have to knock on anybody's door. Of course, as a performer made more money, he was able to live better.

JD. What about traveling, Benny?

BR. In the early days when we traveled, we went by train. If the trip was overnight we sat up all night, and that was that. A little later on, when I was in burlesque, I found a guy who was willing to share an upper berth with me. Well, it was my first time in an upper berth and we got frozen up there. It was murderous, especially when one had to go to the 'john.'

So I determined that I was going to save my dough and some-day get a drawing room. Well, it didn't happen that fast. I kept sleeping in uppers, but always with a hot water bottle at my feet. From there I graduated to a lower, then to a room-ette, then a compartment, and eventually to the drawing room. Of course, there were some circuits where the theatres were so close together that the trips were made by trolley.

JD. When did you get into vaudeville?

BR. My first decent vaudeville would have been in 1920. In 1927 I got a motion picture contract, but I had an understanding that I was to be told well ahead of time when the movies would cut production, so that I could run out and play the vaudeville. You see, all motion picture contracts were forty weeks out of the fifty-two, and they were in command of when the layoffs would be. Sometimes it would be for three days or six days, for example. So, with this understanding that I had, I was able to take my leave from MGM and run back and play the Palace and play Chicago and other places. I did this until 1932. That was when the Palace died, and when the Palace died, bigtime vaudeville died. What was left was called vaudeville but it certainly wasn't bigtime. You see, in bigtime we did two performances a day and the audience sat in reserved seats. But then we got into what we called the presentation, the motion picture houses, where we did four shows a day, along with the movie. Those seats were not reserved and some people sat through several shows. Those presentation houses became horrible grinds, even though the salaries were better than in bigtime vaudeville. I for one hated my own voice. You see, when you walked on the stage of a presentation house, there was always a band, usually set right on the stage in full view of the audience. During the first show the band laughed at the jokes. The second time around, they'd heard the jokes and don't laugh so much. Well, the audience is looking at them. The audience says that if they're not laughing, why should I laugh? By the third show one guy is cleaning his trumpet and the other is fixing the slide on his trombone and another guy's writing a letter, and by the fourth show they hated your guts. The only way I cured that was to switch gags and change shows so that I wouldn't lose those people. But when you're doing that four times a day and five on Saturday and Sunday, seven days a week, then it was really no longer show business. There was nothing artistic about what you did. The performer went on and beggared so many minutes with so many jokes. But it was a lot of money and I did that for as long as I could and then switched over to night clubs. I had played some night clubs intermittently and liked the idea of having all day to myself. Usually there are two shows at night, although at the Chez Paree in Chicago, they had three. As fancy as the Chez Paree sounded, three shows there were murder. I got a log of money there, believe me, I did, but that third show went on about 3:15 in the morning and, as the Emcee, I had to open and close it. The show ran over an hour. By the time I changed clothes and got out of there it was almost five o'clock. Well, night clubs finally became a real drag and I thought the hell with it and I went back to Hollywood and pictures and radio. By that time television had started and I've been here in Hollywood ever since.

JD' Was there talk among vaudevillians, Benny, about retirement, or did you people just decide that your life was acting and that's what you would do till the end?

BR. I believe that all but a few just wanted to keep right on going. There were a couple who were smart enough, and I wasn't one of them, who set a goal for themselves and invested intelligently in order to reach their goal. Some bought annuities and said they would work until they had $25,000 or $50,000, and then they'd retire. But for all those who did that I can think of only one couple that did retire. A lot of acts reached their goals but just kept on going because bigtime vaudeville was beautiful and there was no sense leaving it. Why quit? Where would they go? Look at Jack Benny today. Everybody says to Jack that with all his money and so and so, why doesn't he retire? He says, where am I going? I can't play golf seven days a week, or even seven days a month, he says. Jack just answers that when they put him in the box, he'll retire.

JD. In your vaudeville career, were there particularly tough places to play?

BR. Well, the first one that a performer hated, and all vaudevillians knew that it would be on their route and they'd have to play it, was in New York City, a theatre called the Colonial. Believe me, you could have just played the Palace, or the Alhambra, or any of the bigtime houses around New York, and the audiences were great. The Colonial was murder. There was a certain type of audience in there—let's call them a wise guy audience—and they just dared you. It was known that if you paid a certain guy, he would bring people in to laugh and applaud. It was that kind of joint. Then, Kansas City was murder. In Kansas City there sat the nicest people that you ever saw in your life, in their reserved seats, ladies and gentlemen, and you heard no laughter and very little applause. After the show they'd tell the manager, a wonderful little guy named Lehman, that it had been a beautiful show, one of the best they'd ever seen, but you'd never know it by the way they acted inside the theatre. There was only one guy that I ever heard them laugh at and I was on the bill with him. Now, appreciate who was on the bill at the same time. The Marx Brothers were on the bill and got very few laughs. But this guy made that audience scream—Chic Sale. And, of course, there were hate towns, which you found down South, where they hated Catholics, blacks, and Jews. So anybody like that didn't have a chance. They hated your guts right away.

JD. Benny, I'm presently living near Minneapolis. What about that audience?

BR. The Orpheum, in bigtime vaudeville, was a great audience because of the reserved seat. But the minute the reserved seat was eliminated, then it became a different audience and they were but lousy. They were awful. But when the reserved seat holders were in the theatre, it was fine, and Minneapolis was a great show town in every way.

JD. What about the theatre managers, Benny?

BR. Well, they were dictators and you had to do what they said. They also hated the performer's guts—and there was a reason for that. In the early vaudeville a single act on the bill—by that, I mean that he was a single guy—would get 175 or 200 bucks. A team would get 250 or 300. A headliner, and remember that this is many years ago, would get $1,000 a week. That was a lot of money! Very few people got that kind of pay. So, in those good old days of vaudeville, the end of the week would come and the manager paid us in cash. So, here was a guy giving you $500 or $1,000 a week for telling jokes and he'd got sixty bucks. How can he like you? He's got to hate you! And carry that on, for there were stagehands who hated the performer for the same reason, and even orchestra leaders. Some of them hated you because they realized that they were musicians and had worked many years to become expert in their craft, and they thought to themselves that there was a louse up there on stage, telling some stinking jokes, and getting paid ten times the money they were getting. Incidentally, that was the only hate I knew around vaudeville. At the same time, to be sure, not all managers, stagehands, or orchestra leaders were like that.

JD. What about family life for the vaudeville performer?

BR. Well, everybody was different. Some guys were married but left their wives at home. Those guys who were married and who brought along wives who were not performers just had to come home broke. Wives in that case were referred to as 'excess baggage.' You see, it cost a lot of money for railroad fares, and one in a hotel is a lot different than two in a hotel. Besides that, they had to eat in restaurants. So, in cases like that, everything was tough. Of course, the guy who goes on the road for twenty, thirty, forty, or fifty weeks at a time, and who sends his dough home, sometimes comes back to no home at all. Or if he has one child, or two or three, his children just don't know who he is. They say it makes the grass grow longer or something. It was always best to marry an actress, so that she could share your life with you.

JD. What about those show business families, Benny? Would you say that their relationships were better than if they had been everyday working families?

BR. There's no question about it and I'll give you one quick reason. Most small acts had an unwritten law, that the minute the family was offstage they would not talk to each other until they had taken their makeup off, had dressed, and gone out to eat. If these family acts had not followed that rule, then one would have said that someone else had screwed up some lines or missed a cue, and there would have been hell to pay. So, by this unwirtten law, there are no words spoken until they're on their way out of the theatre, and by that time everyone has calmed down. Now, they get along the best.

JD. What about the sex life of a performer on the road? Did the vaudevillian seek it out from the town girls or prostitutes or just what?

BR. Well, here, too, everybody was different. I'll give you me quick. I always paid. I had come from what could be called an underworld background and I either knew the local bookmaker or I knew where to find him. I'd just tell them that I wanted some service and they'd see to it. The lady would visit my hotel, she'd be paid, and go home. Of course, there were those guys who flirted with waitresses and with chambermaids, and sooner or later they had to wind up in trouble.

JD. What about the female performers?

BR. If the female performer wanted sex she had to find it right on the bill with her. And if she broke up a married couple, she broke them up, because if she couldn't find a single guy on the bill, that's what she had to do. If she wanted sex, she was not going to wait a year till she got back home to whoever the hell she left back there, and that poor sucker, that husband of hers, is in big trouble. I saw it and I saw it and I saw it.

JD. What about food, Benny?

BR. That all depends on where you were and what kind of places you went to. Now, the first thing you'd expect me to say was that the minute I got into a town I looked for a Jewish restaurant. Well, that's exactly where I didn't want to go! And for good reasons, because if you wanted a steak, you can't get it in a Jewish restaurant because they fry all their meats. And even if you loved what was served in a Jewish restaurant—and I even do now, a dish like chopped chicken liver, for example—it's got to kill you with all that *schmaltz* in there. You know what *schmaltz* is—it's chicken fat. Sure, it tastes great, it's wonderful, but it's got to knock you off. What I did when I got into a town was to find the finest Chinese restaurants. I'd go in and just order one thing first, a shrimp roll or an egg roll, and if I liked that I ordered the rest of the meal. If I didn't like it, I paid for it and got out of there. But most Chinese restaurants were best because they didn't serve anything that was from yesterday. It was made fresh, right then. After the Chinese restaurants I would look over the German cooking, for it was mostly roasted meat. But a lot depended on the region. In New England the food was great. You didn't have to worry about it at all because New Englanders fried very little. They had their New England boiled dinners and their lobster and that food was just out of this world. When you were in Chicago, well, that was the best meat in the world, bar no place at all. But you couldn't say that for the Middle West. They ship their best meat out of the country. They still had some pretty good stuff, though, but certainly not the best. And Texas is a question of if you liked fried and fried and fried and fried. Of course, in the beginning, before I knew any better, what the hell, it was fried, fried, fried just about everywhere. But the worst food, as far as I'm concerned, was in the fancy hotels. They tried to give it to you fancy. Simple, good food —they had to put some cockamamie sauce or something on it.

JD. What about black performers, Benny? I won't question the brotherhood on the stage or backstage, but what about outside the theatre? Where did he go? Where did he stay?

BR. He didn't stay with the whites because he couldn't get a hotel with the whites. But those of us who worked with him, we played golf with him, we ate with him, we worked on stages with him, we worked at baseball games with him. It didn't make any difference to us. Only once or twice did I ever see a white man or woman, on the same bill with a black, brush them off. They were Southerners and when they treated the black like that, the rest of us on the bill ignored the white guy. We made their life miserable for them. But there was never anything about black or Jew or Catholic, Protestant, or any kind of religion that could be called prejudice. The only kind of hate that I saw had nothing to do with religion or skin color, and that was during the war. And I was one of the non-intelligent ones who did this, too. We hated Germans who might have been in the war. They could have been lovely people, acrobats, musicians, clowns, anything, but a stupid ass like me would say, you German sonofabitch. But the funny part of that is when they would come into the theatre for rehearsal. This would be at nine o'clock in the morning and everybody's there, rehearsing their music, not their act. These Germans would wait until everybody was on stage and then they'd open the stage door and very loudly would say, 'Doorman, do you got any mail for the Patricks?' (Rubin used a very heavy German accent when speaking that sentence.) Or they'd walk around the theatre singing, 'Oh lee oh lay ee, oh lay ee. Ve are Sviss.'

JD. Could you contrast some of the vaudeville circuits for me, Benny?

BR. Well, let's start in the East. When you broke in an act or when you started as a youngster, you had to play the small-time. When I started I did eight shows a day. There was a motion picture along with that which ran two reels. There were many smalltime circuits in the East, the Poli Time out through Connecticut and part of New England, the Delany Time around Pennsylvania, and there was what was called Fatty Marcus. This guy booked one-nighters or two or three days. When he paid you, we used to say that he paid us off with old programs and baked apples. In other words he didn't pay very much money. He operated little joints around New York. That was about as low as you could get, just like the Butterfield Time. When I say low, I don't mean as a person. What I mean is that performers on the Butterfield had to be about as untalented as you could get, because that was the smallest of the smalltime.

JD. What about the so-called Crescent Circuit?

BR. That was a big nothing. Nothing, nothing. It's somebody stuck a name on some toilets, as we called it. Nothing.

JD. What about the contrast of life on the bigtime?

BR. Well, that was the best show business I knew at the time and I would relish it right now. The opening act went on about 2:20 and only did six or seven minutes. He was out of the theatre by 2:30. This guy could go to a ball game or go out and play golf that afternoon, or go to a million places and still have time to come home, take a nap, eat dinner, and be back in the theatre. Let's take the guy like me, the next-to-closing guy.[2] I went on around five-something and I got off at 5:30. Well, I left the theatre and had a fine dinner and I had the whole evening. I could go to a show or whatever was playing that night and still get to my own theatre in time for my act during the evening show, or in the morning I could play golf as long as I'd want and take a nap afterward. So, this was the finest kind of living. And during those headline days, I got up to $7,500 a week. And yet I will tell you of a show business where I got $16 a week that I liked better than that, and that was on the showboat. Just let me give you one day on the showboat. Breakfast was between eight and ten and, brother, you never missed breakfast because there was ham and eggs and bacon and hot cakes and German fried potatoes, we used to call them, and milk, and we didn't pay for that at all. This was the sixteen and cakes I told you about before. Well, you finish eating and it's 11:30 or 12 o'clock. If you're at a town, maybe you'd take a walk into town or the guys on the boat played pinochle or you fished or you wrote letters or you read books or you sat around and kidded or you rehearsed, but you had all of this leisure. You did the first show at seven. Usually you were in a little bitty town that will have only enough people for two performances. So you did a show at seven and another one at nine. In order to stay in that town a week, you changed your show every day, or if it was too small, you moved on to the next town. But back to the showboat day. Now, the last show is over. It's around 10:30. Now comes that big night lunch, as we called it. And there was a festive board like no Waldorf-Astoria could make up. I don't care where you eat in the world, nobody could set a better table than we on the showboat could, we little stinking actors. It was glorious! Well, the crew had already eaten and, while we ate, the captain got the boat underway. So we went down the river, you're through eating, a guy busted out with an accordion, or sometimes a guitar, and you sat on the top deck and you sang old songs. I don't know any living like this and I would take it tomorrow if somebody would give it to me. That was the greatest show business I ever knew.

JD. What about movies or television?

BR. As far as now, the difference between motion pictures and television is such that you have to pick motion pictures. Take a show like "Gunsmoke," for example. They have to knock that off in five-and-a-half or six days, so you're not going to get too many chances at a scene. If it's lousy, they're going to print, see? But if you're doing a movie, you could stink that scene up twenty, thirty times, and they won't print it unless it's perfect. If anybody makes a lousy picture, they should be horsewhipped because of the time they have and the money they have to do it with. But the showboat was better.

JD. What of the expression, 'The show must go on'? Have you any memories of when that really did apply, Benny?

BR. Yes, and it tore my guts out. At this particular time I was in a vaudeville theatre and I got a wire that my brother, George, passed away. The manager gave me that telegram before the show. Well, if I had walked off that show—I was the headliner—that show was no good, because I also emceed that show. There was nobody who could jump in and replace me in that particular kind of a show, and so I walked on and I did what I had to do. My guts were--you know, what happened to me, you know what my heart must have been, but that show had to go on. I had the same thing happen in a night club called the Casanova, in Detroit. I got the same kind of wire, that my brother, Abe, passed away. And I talked with the owner and he says, 'Benny, if you don't want to go on, we'll explain it.' I says you can't do that, I said you got people here who spent a lot of money in this club, and it's not just for the money, but what do you do for them the rest of the night that they're in here? You say, here's an actor and his brother died, he can't go on, you put a damper on the whole joint, no other actor can make good, you've saddened the room, who're they going to laugh at? So that show had to go on. And I got the same thing when I played the Chanticleer in Baltimore, when my father passed away. I went on and after the show I called my mother and I said I got the wire about Papa and that I'd try to get out of Baltimore by the next day. She said, 'What for? What can you do for him? You're in a business where you're making people happy and you know that show is going to go on, Benny, and you go on!' And those are my three experiences where the show must go on.

JD. Those times must really have been shattering. What about the relationship among performers, Benny? Was there continual great rapport?

BR. Well, you had things like this, where a man and wife had a fight just before they went on the stage. Well, they still went on and did their act. And even if they had to kiss, they kissed. Then, when they came offstage they called each other dirty bastards, sonofabitch, and everything. There were a lot of arguments, too, among boy and girl dance teams. That was a strenuous act and he would say, you flew up in my arms wrong, I tore a muscle, or I hurt my ass, or something, and she would say, the way you grabbed me you hurt me, and they would go on hating each other's guts. The most famous, if you will, was McIntyre and Heath, very big stars, but they disliked each other. They were blackface and were in vaudeville for about twenty minutes until Ziegfeld found them. From then on they were Broadway stars. But they didn't like each other offstage and did not speak for twenty-five or thirty years, which was not really that difficult, because they had separate dressing rooms. They walked on stage, did what they had to do, went back into their separate dressing rooms, and never had a social life. In contrast with this I think the best of them all was Smith and Dale, the 'Dr. Kronkheit' sketch. These guys were together from the time they were twelve years old till they were eighty years of age. They never failed to come off the stage where Charley didn't say, 'Again, you loused up that joke. You don't know how to tell a joke. When the hell are you ever going to learn?' And Joe would say, 'I'll learn if you were a professional and you knew how to do a straight line where a comic could get a laugh. You stink, you sonofabitch.' And they'd go into their dressing rooms and while they took their makeup off, they called each other everything. The minute they were washed and dressed, very quietly Joe would say to Charley, 'Where do you want to eat tonight?' And that was the end.

JD. What about those dressing rooms, Benny? I've read some very bad descriptions of them.

BR. Well, it all depends on where you were. In some towns there wasn't any such thing as a dressing room. You'd come into a basement, a stinking, lousy basement, one toilet, with one bowl to wash up in, and more or less a blanket or a big sheet, the ladies on this side, the men on the other side. Now, this is way back in the beginning. Later on there was stinking one rooms and some had none, and there you made up in the hotel. I even played places where we had to put our makeup on in our railroad car. Then you walked or took a horse and buggy and got to the theatre the best way you could. I remember Amarillo, Texas, when I first played there. The train pulled in and I put on my makeup. There was mud everywhere. They didn't have anything that could be called streets, but I had to get to that stinking, lousy theatre. Well, what you did, you went in your bare feet, you carried your shoes and stockings, and a towel around your neck, and you got to this so-called theatre, you wiped your feet, you put your shoes and stockings on, the footlights, which were what we call Coleman lamps, went up and you went out and did your act. Later on when Albee[3] remodeled the bigtime theatres, each dressing room had this: the most beautiful closets, and a very comfortable--even better than a chaise lounge--thing to relax in. There was a Green Room for actors to sit around and talk and play billiards or pool, if you will. There was a place for people on the bill to wash their clothes and iron them, and that's really when the bigtime was the bigtime. Of course, you have to remember that most of us sent our laundry out, but there were certain things in costumes when laundries would kill you, especially the overnights, you know. What the hell, they'd starch what they shouldn't starch, they'd rip things, and so most girls did their own washing and ironing. In my old H & M trunk, there was a place for an iron and for everything, really. Today, of course, when I do a television show, it's really something. The dressing rooms there have beautiful mirrors, have almost a bed, and they're air-conditioned and even have a telephone.

JD. Well, Benny, this has been a profitable day for me. Thank you very much.

The editing of the tape-recording eliminated material which ranged over many show business areas, yet the essence remains.

NOTES

[1] The tape-recording and full transcript is in the possession of the author.

[2] Next-to-closing was the most important position on a vaudeville bill. When his act finished, only one act remained, an act which very often played to a rapidly emptying theater.

[3] Edward F. Albee was probably the single, most powerful administrator in vaudeville history, in charge of the greatest vaudeville circuit in the nation.

INDEX

New York Stock Exchange, 169
Nigger Nate (Nate Bernstein), 125
"Nino," 140
No Foolin, 19
Norton, Ned, 34

O'Brien, Dolly, 140
O'Brien, Jay, 138, 139, 140, 141
Ocean Park Theatre, 70, 71
O'Donnell, Bob, 38
Ohio River, 23
Olson, George, 173
Oppenheimer, Jess, 159
"Orange Julius," 117, 118
Original Orpheum Theatre in Los
    Angeles, 127
Orpheum, 133, 192
Orpheum Circuit, 33, 74, 67
Orpheum Theatre, 36, 40, 67, 69, 75
Orsatti, Ernie, 105
Orsatti, Vic, 105
Orth, Frank, 95
"Orth and Codee," 95
"Over the Rainbow," 56

Pacific Ocean, 146
Palace Building, 124
Palace Theatre, The, 36, 37, 53, 73, 77,
    78, 80, 91, 167, 171, 172, 173
Paley, William S., 189
"Pals," 171
"Panama Hattie," 176
Pantages Circuit, 25, 40, 191
"paper hangers, the," 36
Paris, France, 95, 96
Park Central Hotel, 152
Parkyakarkas, 180, 185
Parsons, Louella, O., 68, 69, 70, 71, 72
Peabody, Eddie, 71
Pearl, Jack, 78, 79, 80
Pearl, Winnie, 78, 79, 80
Penner, Joe, 34
Pennington, Ann, 144
Percy, Eileen, 145
Peters, Jane, 144
Phalen, Jimmy, 105

Philadelphia, Pa., 33, 42, 45, 81, 113
Pickford, Jack, 129
Pickford, Mary, 129, 192
Pierre Hotel, 78
Pittsburgh, Pa., 33, 42, 53, 153
Porcassi, Frank, 152
Portland "Beavers," 129
Powell, Dick, 105, 106, 185
Power, Tyrone, Sr., 133
Powers "Elephants," 16, 35
Puente, 73
President Coolidge, 135
Prevost, Marie, 129
Princeton Hotel, 30, 31, 42
Providence, Rhode Island, 47
Pulley, B. S., 39
Purviance, Edna, 129
Putnam Building, 133

Raft, George, 105, 106, 130
Rath Brothers, 24
Ratoff, Gregory, 78, 120, 121
Raymond, Miss (of Dugan and
    Raymond), 104
"Red," 77, 78
"Red Cross," 74
Red Dust, 192
Reeves, Daniel, 166, 167, 168
Reisenweber's Cafe, 31
Retter, Dezzo, 24, 89
Reno, Nevada, 99
"Reuben Reuben I Been Thinkin," 91
Reynolds, Abe, 75
Richmond, Va., 32
Rickles, Don, 63
Ritz Brothers, 105, 106, 168
Ritzy Rosie, 71
R.K.O., 179
Roberti, Lyda, 69
Robinson, Dewey, 106
Rogell, Al, 182
Rogell, Sid, 179, 180, 182, 185
Rogers, Buddy, 192
Rogers, Ginger, 176
Rogers, Will, 16
Rognan, Lorraine, 30